THE PAINFUL PATH OF A PRODIGAL

BIBLICAL HELP AND HOPE FOR THOSE WHO LOVE THE WAYWARD AND REBELLIOUS

THE PAINFUL PATH
OF A PRODIGAL

BIBLICAL HELP AND HOPE FOR THOSE WHO
LOVE THE WAYWARD AND REBELLIOUS

CRAIG K. SVENSSON

"A powerful and heartbreaking story that is real, raw, and yet full of gospel centered hope. This book belongs in every pastor and biblical counselor's library. I have watched Craig and Sue walk this path and I praise the Lord for the strength and grace he has given and continues to give. I believe our redeeming God will use this marvelous book to draw prodigals to himself and comfort and sustain parents who find themselves on this difficult journey."
—Pastor Steve Viars, D.Min, Senior Pastor of Faith Church, Lafayette IN, author of *Putting Your Past in its Place* and *Loving Your Community*

"In *The Painful Path of a Prodigal*, Craig Svensson has written a very moving and very needed book with a unique perspective for parents of prodigal children. While clearly hope-giving, this book is also filled with biblical candor and lament. And, as the subtitle indicates—*Biblical Help and Hope for Those Who Love the Wayward and Rebellious*—Craig shares wisdom for parenting life. Craig's biblical counsel reminds me of Philippians 1:9-10: 'And this is my prayer: that your love may abound more and more in knowledge and depth of insight, so that you may be able to discern what is best and may be pure and blameless for the day of Christ.'"
—Bob Kellemen, Ph.D., VP/Academic Dean at Faith Bible Seminary, Lafayette, IN, and Author of *Raising Kids in the Way of Grace*

"In *The Painful Path of a Prodigal*, Craig has written an indispensable book for those enduring the sorrow, grief, and confusion of dealing with prodigal children. For family members or friends of prodigals, questions multiply. From the heart of a father who intimately understands the myriad of incredibly difficult issues that arise, the reader will find practical, hopeful direction to navigate this arduous journey well. Craig's insightful book addresses common situations with clarity, care, discernment, and biblical wisdom. I enthusiastically recommend this book for anyone in the midst of the deep suffering that attends loving a prodigal."
—Pamela Gannon, RN, MABC, ACBC certified Biblical Counselor at Grace Bible Church, Adjunct faculty at Montana Bible College, Bozeman, MT; Coauthor with Beverly Moore of *In the Aftermath: Past the pain of Childhood Sexual Abuse*

"With wisdom born from experience and careful consideration of biblical truth, Dr. Craig Svensson offers compassionate hope and help to parents facing the difficult reality of a wayward child. Furthermore, for pastors, counselors, mentors, and friends of the parents of prodigals, Dr. Svensson's work should be the first resource they read to provide the most helpful guidance during this life-consuming trial."
—BRENT AUCOIN, Ph.D., Pastor of Seminary and Soul Care Ministries, Faith Church, Lafayette, IN

"In my years serving young women through biblical counseling, I have often been confronted with the devastating effects that one person's rebellious choices can have. In addition to the challenging counseling required for the young lady caught in the tangle of her sin's consequences, I frequently was called on to offer many additional hours of help to the friends and family of that prodigal. While we believe God always uses the sinful choices of others to further refine and grow us, navigating specific internal and external responses that are loving but righteous is a challenge. I am thrilled to now have a book like this that can be offered in those difficult moments. As only one who has previously walked this tragic path can, Dr. Svensson humbly and hopefully offers true biblical counsel, comforting even while he challenges the reader to love and serve like Jesus in heartbreaking situations."
—JOCELYN WALLACE, Inaugural Executive Director at Vision of Hope Residential Treatment Center, Lafayette, IN

To our gracious Creator, who gives "beauty for ashes, the oil of joy for mourning, the garment of praise for the spirit of heaviness"

ISAIAH 61:3, KJV

CONTENTS

PREFACE

This book did not begin from a well-crafted plan. Its origin remains somewhat mysterious to me. It began on a cold winter night several weeks after our prodigal son's tragic death. Due to several chronic illnesses, sleep has often been elusive to me over the last twenty years. But in the early weeks after our son's death, sleep was frequently beyond my grasp. Every time I closed my eyes, I saw images of the photos shown to me by members of the county coroner's office. It seemed as though the photo of his pale dead face was etched on my inner eyelids.

Rather than continuing to toss and turn, and risk disturbing my wife's sleep, I slinked with the stealth of a cat to my writing room—intending to work on a book about living with chronic illness that I had begun in preparation for an upcoming sabbatical leave from my university. I rubbed my hands together to warm my fingers as I waited for my laptop to complete its magical process of coming alive. Inexplicably, rather than opening the file of my early book draft, I created a new document and began to type. From my mind to my fingers flowed elements of our story on a fifteen- year journey with a prodigal son who descended into the depths of drug abuse and its associated problems. Over the ensuing weeks, I continued to write about the biblical lessons we learned through our journey. I cannot explain why. I simply felt compelled to write. I am not sure when my thoughts turned from personal journaling to writing a book. Upon our son's death, my wife and I embraced Isaiah 61:3 as a personal prayer—specifically, that God would give "beauty for ashes, the oil of joy for mourning, the garment of praise for the spirit of heaviness." In whatever ways possible, we asked him to turn this tragedy into a means of good for others. The time came when I began to pray and ask if perhaps the Lord might have me share our experiences with others, and the lessons we learned, in order to help them in their time of affliction. The thoughts of making our personal story so public was scary. Still, could I fulfill the call of 2 Corinthians 1:3–5 and share the comfort we received with others in need of comfort? Indeed, was it a biblical obligation?

My dear wife was taken aback when I first told her of my compulsion to write and to consider sharing our experience with others. I gave her a draft with the promise that not another soul would see it unless she was comfortable with my doing so. It took her about a month to generate the fortitude to begin reading the first page. Sometime later, with her cheeks drenched with tears, she said "Yes, you need to share this with others."

Parents of prodigals struggle deeply with the challenges they face in relating to their wayward offspring. Siblings, spouses, and children of prodigals face similar struggles. How do you live for Christ in the midst of such personal turmoil? How do you live with a grown child whose destructive choices have turned them into a person so unlike the adorable offspring into whom you poured much of yourself? Ultimately, how do you bear the pain if they never return?

As a visiting seminary lecturer, interim preacher, and Bible teacher, I have taught the Word of God to pastors and pastors-in-training, mature and immature believers, children and adults, as well as audiences of skeptics. As a professor and dean of one of the top pharmacy schools in the nation, I have taught students in a variety of health professions the proper and improper use of drugs as well as conducted extensive research on adverse drug effects. None of these roles prepared me to be the parent of a prodigal who descended into the depths of substance abuse and its associated destructive behaviors. But this difficult journey forced me to search the Scriptures for guidance.

Loved ones of prodigals often feel overwhelmed and isolated. Too often, their faith becomes unmoored. My goal is to help anchor the faith of parents, siblings, spouses, and offspring struck by the storms their prodigal creates. I also hope to help a group untouched by other authors—loved ones of a prodigal who never returns. Grounded in the truth of Scripture, family members of prodigals can know inner joy and serve as a light for Christ at a time when they feel their world is collapsing around them. The goal of this book is to help those loved ones use Scripture as their guide in facing the difficult, and often perplexing issues arising from engaging with those who have abandoned themselves to reckless living. If it achieves this goal, we will give thanks for the exchange of "beauty for ashes."

1

THE END OF THE JOURNEY

Having forewarned me it would be difficult to look at, the man slid a photo across my office conference table. I forced my eyes to look down at the image. There was no need to gaze long upon the face. My heart wanted to deny it was he. However, those were clearly his eyes. The nose as I had seen it since his birth. Though his overall features were distorted, there was no denying who the picture captured. Gripped by this reality, I raised my eyes to the man across the table—who sat silent while awaiting my verdict. Deep within I wanted to scream, "I never saw this face before. I do not know who he is." Yet I did. I knew with certainty. My voice cracked as I acknowledged to this visitor from the county coroner's office that the photo had captured my youngest child. The body they found was the boy I once held so tenderly. Thus, just one month after his thirtieth birthday, an end came to a fifteen-year journey of watching his painful descent into drug abuse and its attendant ugliness. Now I knew what my wife and I long feared—our prodigal would never come home.

People find great hope in the story of the prodigal son told by the Lord Jesus. It pictures the gracious love our heavenly Father shows in forgiving all who repent and turn to him. Many a follower of Jesus whose child chose a path of sinful living have clung to the hope their child's story would have a similar glorious ending. Untold numbers have returned in repentance and to restoration. We join the angels in heaven praising God for each who returned. But many have not. Many never did, nor ever will.

How do you live the abundant life Jesus promised when the shadow of a prodigal who never returned follows you for the remaining days of your life? You might conclude my wife and I began to learn those lessons the day the coroner visited my university office with photos of our son. In fact, those lessons began during the journey, while hope remained. Though difficult, they prepared us for living when the time for hope was past.

Not all children who wander from the faith are prodigals. Some offspring are not walking with the Lord, but are otherwise upstanding citizens in the eyes of society. They hold gainful employment, fulfill parental duties well, and are good neighbors. Their spiritual well-being is a concern. They need prayer, the truth spoken in love, and the effectual work of the Spirit in their life. Nevertheless, such do not fit the category of prodigal as presented by Jesus. While the word prodigal does not appear in the Bible, most people with a knowledge of Scripture identify it with the son in this parable. The word itself derives from the Latin *prodigus*, meaning "wasteful."[1] Consider how Jesus describes such an individual:

> There was a man who had two sons. And the younger
> of them said to his father, "Father, give me the share
> of property that is coming to me." And he divided
> his property between them. Not many days later, the
> younger son gathered all he had and took a journey into
> a far country, and there he squandered his property in
> reckless living.
> **Luke 15:11–13**

This young man rejected the path on which his father led him, giving himself over to a life of sin. He did the unthinkable in asking for his inheritance while his father remained alive. Receiving the goods, he bundled them up and journeyed far away. He violated all cultural norms of familial fidelity.[2] In apparent short order, his chosen path led to his ruin. Coming to his senses, he returned home to the father he had previously spurned.

This book is not about the well-adjusted but lost offspring—

---

1   Online Etymology Dictionary, www.etymonline.com.

2   For a discussion of the cultural context of this parable, see Kenneth E. Bailey, *The Cross & the Prodigal: Luke 15 Through the Eyes of Middle Eastern Peasants. 2nd Edition* (Downers Grove, Il.: InterVarsity Press, 2005).

though his eternal need is just as great.[3] This work is for those who are living, or have lived, with one who has abandoned himself to reckless living—a prodigal in the truest sense of the word. It is for the many whose loved one has entered a downward spiral, shattering relationships, incurring judicial action, destroying trust, and molding your beloved into a stranger you hardly know anymore.

At the same time, loved ones do not become prodigals overnight. There are serious heart issues that evolve before someone enters into full-bore rebellion and embraces a reckless lifestyle. Hence, many of the biblical principles covered in the chapters ahead are relevant for those whose loved one has started down a descending path, but has not yet outright rejected the road on which you would lead them.

Living through the difficult years with a prodigal was excruciatingly painful and often confusing. We faced difficult choices unimagined by parents whose children never wandered far from the faith. The challenge of the choices faced is painfully real for those who journey down this hard road. If your loved one is still alive and remains far from the faith, you should hold on to hope they will be a prodigal who one day returns. Our God delights in bringing rebellious souls into his forever family. So, continue to pray earnestly for their return. We prayed this way for fifteen years. Tragically, our story did not end as desired. Nevertheless, we learned much during this heartbreaking journey. We are grateful for how the Lord used it to humble us and cause us to cling to him more closely. Despite the pain, we can praise God for the fruit born from a hard road. A very hard road.

This book is for those with a prodigal (or one started on this path) or those who wish to help them (e.g., pastors, counselors). Some living with a prodigal are not the parent. They are the siblings, spouses, or even children of prodigals. Though somewhat different in their experience, many of the difficult issues are similar for all that are related to a prodigal. I write from the perspective of a parent and, therefore, refer to the prodigal as an offspring or child. But the biblical applications are relevant for

---

3 For simplicity, singular references to a prodigal in this book use the masculine. This does not negate the reality of female prodigals.

all who engage those on this destructive path. There is also some explicit discussion in later chapters for spouses of prodigals. I earnestly hope to help those who travel with prodigals think biblically as they march through their journey.

I also hope to fill the void of help for those whose prodigal will never return. It occurs more frequently than many would acknowledge. But there is much hope and help in the Word of God—even for those whose prodigal will never return.

If you are looking for a book to offer a path certain to bring your prodigal to Christ, you will be disappointed. There is no formula to assure repentance and restoration. But I will help you understand why this is true. If you join me through the pages ahead, I will turn the light of Scripture on some of the most difficult issues faced by parents and other family members of prodigals, issues such as: As a parent of a prodigal, how do I deal with the judgment of others? How do I live with my failures as a parent or spouse of a prodigal? When is it loving to let go and allow the prodigal to bear the full consequences of their destructive choices? Why do children become prodigals? How do I battle the anger my prodigal can often provoke within me? How do I have confidence in my prayer life when prayers for my prodigal go unanswered? Is God's grace sufficient for the trial through which I am walking? These and other questions are the focus in subsequent chapters.

You will benefit most by closing the book at the end of each chapter to think and pray. Every situation is unique. You need God's wisdom to know the right steps in your journey. Take the time to seek it. If you are the parent of a prodigal, I would encourage you to read this book aloud with your spouse—with an open Bible as your companion. As parents, you will tend to respond emotionally to the many challenges presented by your prodigal. Together, you need to learn to think biblically about these issues, and filter your emotions through biblical truth. If you are the adult sibling of a prodigal, I would encourage you also to read it aloud with your spouse, if you are married. Your spouse may not have an emotional bond with your prodigal sibling, but you need to agree on how you will respond to the issues they bring into your relationship. If you are an unmarried child of a prodigal, you may find help in reading it aloud with your believing parent—if this is practical. The believing parent will need your support in special ways. In like manner, you will need their help in processing the challenging issues introduced into your family by a prodigal parent.

Some truths to be considered in the pages ahead may be hard to hear. At times, Scripture paints a painful picture of reality. Jesus taught some hard things—not hard in the sense of difficult to understand, but hard to receive as truth. Some turned from Jesus when they found his words hard to receive (John 6:60-66). We must neither fear nor shy away from the hard truths of Scripture. Ultimately, the truth will set us free (John 8:32). We must be willing to consider those difficult truths from Scripture—for we know any pain induced is limited to the here and now.

Loved ones of prodigals walk a painful path. It is easy to think comfort will only come by the repentance and restoration of your prodigal. However, if we link our joy solely to the response of the heart of our wandering loved one, the journey will be unbearable and a tragic outcome will be devastating. True joy and comfort can only be found when our hope rests solidly in our heavenly Father. It is to him, through his Word, that we must turn for guidance on this painful journey. Let's allow the light of his Word to help us see how to navigate these difficult waters.

2

LIVING WITH THE JUDGMENT OF OTHERS

He stood the better part of a foot taller than me and approached aggressively with steely determination in his eyes. Apart from his pointer finger, he clenched a raised hand into a fist. While wagging this hand uncomfortably close to my face, with gritting teeth he declared, "The Bible says 'train up a child in the way he should go and when he is old he shall not depart from it.' If your son is rebelling it is your fault and no one else's!" After unleashing his accusation, he stomped off.

Moments earlier, in our church prayer meeting, I had asked for prayer for our son who was rebelling from the way we were leading him. The reaction it generated from this man not only took me by surprise, it also caused me to think twice about sharing our struggles with our church family. It was only the first of many acts of judgment thrown our way from fellow followers of Christ. We learned to dread the judgment of others and, for as long as possible, became silent sufferers. We did not feel safe in our own church family.

Those whose children openly rebel know too well the oft- spoken adage that the church is the only army that shoots its own wounded. My wife and I struggled to understand the aggressive reaction of this brother who threw a Bible verse at me like a javelin. I was appealing for prayers to help us through what would turn out to be a long painful journey. Instead, it provoked an angry and accusatory response. Other heartless comments over the years left us puzzled about why people would so quickly judge fellow believers as parental and spiritual failures, even when the conduct of our other children would suggest otherwise.

Perhaps the answer is that many parents embrace a form of

spiritual determinism. They believe your child will not go astray if you follow key steps in parenting. Many published books contain the notion that, if you follow a set of principles articulated by their author, you will assure a godly heritage. Some believe they have the formula to fix things if you've messed up. Writing to parents of prodigals, one author declared he discovered "principles for getting the prodigal back to God." Certain the problem lies with the parents of prodigals, he stresses the need for parents to change, insisting that "when you do, you will see the change in your prodigal."

My wife was at a women's program where one speaker confidently proclaimed, "If you follow these biblical principles, your son or daughter will not end up in jail." At that moment, our son was in a prison in Iowa. The message seemed to be that his imprisonment resulted from our failure as parents. Not long thereafter, a well-known pastor declared on his radio program, "I have never seen a child depart from the faith where the father was a truly godly man." Without ever speaking to me, this shepherd of Christ's flock declared me ungodly. Maybe both speakers placed an accurate judgment at my feet. God will be my judge on this in a future day. Yet we have known of many couples who journeyed down a similar path with a prodigal, and these couples exhibited a pattern of Christ-honoring conduct as parents.

After our son's death, well-meaning (but misguided) believers made similar off-the-mark comments. Most in our current town did not know our son. Despite this, some came up to us after his death making statements such as, "Surely, with such godly parents your son was a believer." In their minds, the godliness of the parents assured their offspring would embrace the faith. We were unsure if they thought of the inverse relationship—if the child is ungodly, so must be the parents.

The Error of Spiritual Determinism

Spiritual determinism is a comfortable place to land as a parent, unless you have a prodigal. It leaves one with a sense of control—though a false sense to be sure. Who would not want a guarantee that our kids will turn out okay as we take up the challenge of parenting our newborn offspring? The most dangerous element of spiritual determinism is that it feeds our pride. It makes us feel we are in control. It places us in the position of thinking we can determine the outcome of our parenting. Spiritual determinism turns what should be humble obedience to God's precepts into a self-boasting confidence that we can assure that all will turn out right. But it is a lie.

Those who embrace spiritual determinism must deal with some challenging truths from Scripture. For example, where did God go wrong when his first children rebelled? Where did Jesus fail in his discipleship leading Judas to betray him to death? Did Satan and the other angels who rebelled fail to receive proper instruction or example from the Father? We could add those named in Hebrews 11 as commendable models of faith, yet there were many on this list whose offspring departed from the faith. These and other realities from Scripture make spiritual determinism indefensible. The rebellion of others does not mean failure by those responsible for their instruction.

Importantly, the Lord Jesus said faithfulness to the gospel would be a source of division in human relationships—including the family.

Do you think that I have come to give peace on earth?
No, I tell you, but rather division. For from now on in
one house there will be five divided, three against two
and two against three. They will be divided, father against
son and son against father, mother against daughter
and daughter against mother, mother-in-law against
her daughter-in-law and daughter-in-law against her
mother-in-law.
Luke 12:51–53

This division caused by gospel-faithfulness will sometimes bring lethal consequences:
Brother will deliver brother over to death, and the father
his child, and children will rise against parents and have
them put to death.
Matthew 10:21

The words of Jesus are clear: rebellion by children against the gospel will be a part of the experience of some Christian parents because the gospel is a source of division. We respond with sympathy to those whose parents have rejected them because of their faith. For we know, the gospel divides. We pray for a special measure of God's grace for those who experience rejection from a spouse arising from their faith because we know the gospel divides. Jesus said it would also divide parents from their children. Spiritual determinism ignores this plain truth.

BIBLICAL INSTRUCTIONS TO PARENTS

There are passages in Scripture to guide parents on how to raise their children, though there are fewer than one might expect if the following of exact instructions were sure to produce spiritual offspring. Consider the many details given in the Law for the worship of Israel. In comparison, we find few specific instructions about raising children to assure the spiritual well-being of the next generation. The book of Leviticus overflows with intricate instructions on the ceremonial elements of the law, but not one instruction for raising children. Several chapters in Deuteronomy give explicit commands to teach children the law (4:9–10; 6:7; 11:19), but not a word on so many other aspects of parenting that fill modern books on the family. The New Testament is similarly sparse. The focus is being the kind of follower that honors Jesus. It seems one's greatest impact on others—be they neighbors or one's own children—occurs through a life that models the Savior in thought, word, and deed. The explicit instructions on parenting in the New Testament are pointed, but few:

> *"Fathers, do not provoke your children to anger, but bring them up in the discipline and instruction of the Lord."*
> **Ephesians 6:4**

> *"Fathers, do not provoke your children, lest they become discouraged."*
> **Colossians 3:21**

There you have the total of New Testament specific teaching on parenting. Directed at fathers, it provides both a warning and a general path on which to lead one's children: "in the discipline and instruction of the LORD." It provides no promise regarding the outcome. However, it gives a clear focus for paternal responsibility. Ephesians 6:4 declares the responsibility of fathers to provide intentional spiritual instruction for their children. We are to teach them the nature by which the Lord chastens—or disciplines—to mold us into the image of his dear Son. They must hear and see how the Lord uses the circumstances and trials of life as his refining instruments. We are to lay before them the truth of Scripture. They must hear the commandments of the Lord, which we obey as an expression of our love for Jesus (John 14:15). These are the expectations placed upon fathers.

The Old Testament also provides some helpful advice: "Whoever spares the rod hates his son, but he who loves him is diligent to discipline him" (Proverbs 13:24), and "Discipline your son, for there is hope" (Proverbs 19:18). The early chapters of Proverbs provide explicit instruction and warning to sons (though this instruction seems directed to young adults and not children).[4] These and other passages show there is a right way to parent and there are wrong ways to raise the next generation. Nevertheless, the Bible does not support a view of parenting as an unalterable mathematical formula:

Teaching our children rightly

+

living a godly example

=

faithful children

Oh, if only it were so simple!

---

4   It is difficult to conceive that one would warn young children, as opposed to young men, about the dangers of a seductress—as is done in early chapters in Proverbs.

The Meaning of Proverbs 22:6

Many believe that Proverbs 22:6, the passage with which my brother in Christ confronted me, promises that if we raise our children rightly, they will not depart from the faith. Consider what the passage says: "Train up a child in the way he should go; even when he is old he will not depart from it" (Proverbs 22:6).

First, it might be helpful to remember the man believed to have penned this proverb departed from the faith: "For when Solomon was old his wives turned away his heart after other gods, and his heart was not wholly true to the LORD his God, as was the heart of David his father" (I Kings 11:4). Furthermore, we are told "Solomon did what was evil in the sight of the LORD and did not wholly follow the LORD, as David his father had done" (v. 6). In his old age, Solomon himself became a prodigal—one who it appears never returned.

Second, there are other examples of godly kings of Israel whose sons rebelled against the Lord. Consider the case of Josiah. We are told in 2 Kings 23 that "Before him there was no king like him, who turned to the LORD with all his heart and with all his soul and with all his might, according to all the Law of Moses, nor did any like him arise after him" (v. 25). What a remarkable statement about the faithfulness of this king. No king following him exceeded his godliness. Sadly, we learn his son Jehoahaz, who reigned after Josiah's death, "did what was evil in the sight of the LORD" (v. 32). There is also the contrasting picture of the godly King Hezekiah, who "did what was right in the eyes of the LORD, according to all that David his father had done" (2 Chronicles 29:2). Yet this godly man arose from the house of Ahaz—one of the most evil kings in the Davidic line. These and other examples from Scripture should cause one to question a formulaic approach to Proverbs 22:6, wherein following its prescription assures a spiritual prodigy. How then should we view this verse?

No verse should be interpreted in isolation. We must see it in the full context of Scripture. To declare Proverbs 22:6 as deterministic in the spiritual state of one's offspring, you must find Scripture supporting the notion of one person controlling the eternal destiny of another. Of course, Scripture is devoid of support for this view. Consider the experience of the apostle Paul. In Philemon 24, he includes Demas as among those who were his fellow workers. Sadly, he later says, "Demas, in love with this present world, has deserted me" (2 Timothy 4:10). Paul's discipleship was not enough to bind him to a faithful walk. Consider also his passionate appeal for his fellow Israelites: "For I could wish that I myself were accursed and cut off from Christ for the sake of my brothers" (Romans 9:3a). His teaching was not enough to win his fellow Israelites to Christ. The example of the betrayal of Judas—who failed to embrace the offer of the Master that he had followed for over three years—is the most profound example showing that teaching rightly does not assure a faithful disciple. Scripture does not support a view of this passage from Proverbs as assuring a spiritually righteous outcome. What then does this passage mean?

The book of Proverbs is a collection of wisdom to provide instruction to the young and naïve (Proverbs 1:2-6). This book declares the Lord made the world in which we dwell through wisdom (3:19-20). The overall structure and content of Proverbs assumes cause and effect are operational in both the physical and moral realm in which we dwell.[5] If you do such-and-such, this is what will happen. Not always, but most of the time—due to the inherent principle of cause and effect embedded in the order created by God. For example, Proverbs 15:1 tells us "A soft answer turns away wrath." More often than not, this is true. However, most people with a meaningful amount of gray hair on their heads could recount experiences in life where it has not held true. We have encountered angry individuals whose vehemence was unchecked by a soft reply. Even Stephen—whose countenance was viewed by his enemies as like the face of an angel (Acts 6:15)—could not forestall the anger of his opponents with his gracious declaration of truth. The apostle Paul fared no better in a similar situation (Acts 22). Thus, though it is not an absolute, Proverbs 15:1 is a piece of practical wisdom that experience shows we would do well to follow. It is sound advice to the young and immature, as well as the old and forgetful.

---

5   Greg W. Parsons. "Guidelines for Understanding and Proclaiming the Book of Proverbs." Bibliotheca Sacra 150:151-170, 1993.

We should not hear the wisdom sayings of Proverbs as unconditional promises from the Lord.[6] Neither internal evidence from the book itself, nor references to it elsewhere in Scripture, would support such an approach to this valuable portion of the Bible. Hence, "proverbs tell what generally takes place without making an irreversible rule that fits all circumstances." [7]

Seen in this light, Proverbs 22:6 is a truism that should motivate parents to provide intentional instruction for their children. When you teach them rightly, they will follow. Not always, but most of the time. When offspring of Christian parents are not walking in the ways of the Lord, it may reveal parental failure to instruct as the Lord commanded. Alternatively, it may mean their children rejected the instruction and example they were given. In fact, Scripture tells us that more children will choose the path of rejection in the last days (2 Timothy 3:2).

Other interpretations of Proverbs 22:6 seek to remove the contradiction between the declaration that a child will not depart from parental teaching on the things of God and the experience that some children do depart. Each is a recent and minority view with significant deficiencies. One which appears to be growing in popularity posits that the text is sarcastic in nature—as in "train up a child in the way he wants to go (which will surely be to evil), and when he is old he will not depart from that path." Jason DeRouchie, Professor at Bethlehem College and Seminary, has done an admirable job concisely explaining why this interpretation arises from an unsound hermeneutic.[8]

Spiritual determinism is unsupportable when examined in the light of Scripture. As parents, we cannot assure the outcome of our children—for good or bad. This does not mean we should abandon instructing our children. We must teach, both in word and by example. Failure to do so has consequences.

I devoted my professional career to educating future nurses, pharmacists, and physicians. They may fail to gain critical knowledge in two ways. First, *I* could fail to make it a part of

---

6   Gordon D. Fee and Douglas Stuart, *How to Read the Bible for All Its Worth.* (Grand Rapids, Mi.: Zondervan, 1981), 98-99, 203.

7   Parsons, "Guidelines for Understanding," 159.

8   Jason DeRouchie, http://www.desiringgod.org/articles/ train-up-a-child-in-the-way-he-should-go

the content I teach. Second, *they* could refuse to put in the time and energy necessary to learn. I should be held accountable for the first failure, the second is the responsibility of the student. My inability to force them to learn does not mean it is futile for me to teach to the best of my ability—giving careful attention to determining the right content and delivery. Most will learn. The failure of a few does not negate this truth. Nor does it remove my responsibility to teach well.

Parenting is a high calling. We will impact the lives of these young ones in our homes. We have a responsibility before God to do our very best. The uncertainty of the outcome for any specific child does not reduce or remove this responsibility.

RESPONDING TO THE JUDGMENT OF OTHERS

How then should we respond when the painful judgment of others falls upon us? First, we should allow it to humble us. We must realize our sovereign God puts critics in our lives for our good. If the Lord uses the wrongful judgment of others to strike a blow to my pride, I should rejoice as this "enemy within" is losing its grip—whatever the means by which this is accomplished. Any chisel the Lord uses to chip away at my pride is welcome. While there remains far too much pride within us, my wife and I have often spoken of how puffed up we would likely be if all our children were model Christians.

Second, allow the experience to rid you of the fear of man. We worry far too much what others think of us. We often travel down the path of sin because of our desire for admiration from men. Proverbs warns us that "[t]he fear of man lays a snare" (29:25). Walking down this path is akin to stepping into a trap. No man judges rightly, since there is much he doesn't know. Most importantly, others do not know our innermost thoughts and motives. It is best they don't know these things. For if they did, they would think even less of us. The judgment of the Lord should be our only concern (Proverbs 29:25; 1 Corinthians 4:3). Remember the example of Jesus, who "when he suffered, he did not threaten, but continued entrusting himself to him who judges justly" (1 Peter 2:23b).

Third, examine your own life to determine where you have been guilty of judging others. We live in an age where quick and uninformed judgment of others is a common pastime. We are sometimes infected with this ailment ourselves. When experiencing wrongful judgment, look to see where you have wrongly hurled accusations at others. Then repent and learn.

Fourth, return good for evil. When wrongly judged by others, we have the blessed opportunity to model our Savior—who "when he was reviled, he did not revile in return" (1 Peter 2:23a). If we believe they have judged our character wrongly, what better way to make this clear than through a godly response to their accusation? Do not allow their misplaced accusation to cause you to fail in your obligation to "let us do good to everyone" (Galatians 6:10)—including your false accuser.

Fifth, speak the truth in love (Ephesians 4:15). While the time and place must be appropriate, invite them to consider the truth of Scripture with you and to learn about your experience—so they might learn to judge wisely. I failed my brother spoken of earlier on this account. I allowed my sense of personal offense to justify avoiding my obligations toward him in my role as a Bible teacher in our church. Subsequent events revealed he was unprepared to handle his own trials biblically. Might I have helped him if I had taken the difficult move toward him years earlier?

We must realize the Refiner will use even the wrongful judgment of others to rid the dross from our lives. It will be painful, but it will produce sanctification. For this, we can be thankful. The wrongful judgment of others is ultimately for our good when it makes us more like Jesus.

While we experienced our fair share of judgment from others, some believers in our sphere did not feel threatened by our painful journey with our prodigal. They served as a source of great encouragement and tangible help. A few men invested their time and energy to reach our son. Others were just there to show Christian love to him. Each of our pastors have shepherded us well in the most difficult of moments, never leaving us with any sense of judgment from them. We have seen the body of Christ minister well to those dealing with this particular tragedy, and for this, we will be eternally grateful.

We often felt the sting of the judgment of others while our son remained in our home; less so in the years of his living apart from us. We could do nothing about the attitude of others. Learning to leave judgment in the hands of the Lord is the only healthy place to be.

> *But with me it is a very small thing that I should be*
> *judged by you or by any human court.*
> **1 Corinthians 4:3a**

3

EMBRACING FORGIVENESS

A burly deputy from the sheriff's office stood on each side of him with hands gripping his elbows. Dressed in an orange jumpsuit with ankles and hands shackled, the officers further restrained him by handcuffs chained to a thick leather belt around his waist. It was unfathomable to think this was our son the deputies were escorting into the courtroom. Apart from the day of his death, it was our lowest point as parents. As our son shuffled across the courtroom to his position before the judge, troubling questions reverberated through my head. Where did we go wrong? How had we failed as parents that led us to this place? My wife and I wrestled with these questions as we journeyed home from this agonizing court appearance. These and similar questions have risen within us over the years more often than we could count. They have, at times, haunted us. That evening was one of many nights my wife and I had an infant-like experience—crying ourselves to sleep.

Parents of a prodigal wrestle with questions of how their own failures contributed to their child's choice of a wayward path. It is natural to reflect on your parenting and identify things left undone, things you wish you did not do, or things you could have done better. No one who honestly evaluates their parenting will be devoid of areas of regret. Those who have a prodigal are especially prone to blame themselves and their own failures for their child's shortcomings. This can lead to destructive self-blaming, which inevitably harms other relationships in life. Persistent, introspective analysis of one's past parenting is unhealthy and unbiblical. As a parent—or spouse—of a prodigal, how does one deal with these struggles?

ACKNOWLEDGE YOUR IMPERFECTIONS

No parent has always been exemplary in their actions towards their children. There were days when our words to them were wrong, perhaps even destructive. We missed teachable moments because we were preoccupied with lesser things. Our imperfection as parents should not be open for debate. Does this surprise us? Aren't we all imperfect? This is why we groan for the fullness of our redemption that awaits our Savior's return (cf. Romans 8:23). Face the reality, you—like the rest of us—were an imperfect parent. Do not beat yourself up over your imperfection.

Spouses of prodigals may experience similar inner struggles. You will be able to recall moments of failure when you did not behave as you should toward your spouse. This shouldn't surprise you or your spouse. Every marriage brings together two flawed human beings. It is unrealistic to think you would never fail in your desire to be all you should be as a spouse.

David was said to be a man after God's own heart (Acts 13:22), especially and specifically chosen by God. As the Singer of Israel, he penned seventy-three of the psalms—words that have ministered to the children of God for several millennia. Untold numbers of congregations, past and present, give praise to the God of heaven through his words of poetic praise. Despite this, commentators and preachers through the ages have pointed to his parental failures. David's example should remind us that our imperfection as a parent or spouse does not disqualify us for use by God.

CONFESS SINFUL FAILURES

Maybe you examined your parenting and realized not only your imperfections but persistent patterns of sin. It could be you used physical force inappropriately or were prone to yell rather than speak. Conceivably, you neglected your parental responsibility because you gave yourself over to other pursuits. If this is the case, confess your sin to God. Specifically and as plainly as you are able, confessing the sin in the language of biblical truth. Stating, "I wasn't the parent I should have been" is not true confession. Name the sin. "I repeatedly lied—unwilling to acknowledge my sin to my prodigal." "I let sinful anger drive my response more times than I could count." "I abused my power as a parent and exasperated my daughter." "I failed to nurture my children in the ways of the Lord." Where appropriate and possible, confess your sin to those against whom you sinned. Again, as specifically as you can.

If a persistent sinful pattern existed in your parenting, it likely also affects other relationships in your life. You should examine your present life to determine if such patterns remain, then address them where they exist. Have an open and direct conversation with your spouse to deal with residual issues between you. Expand the sphere of confession if needed.

Accept God's Forgiveness

The apostle John penned an important reminder to believers who might struggle with putting past failures behind them: "If we confess our sins, he is faithful and just to forgive us our sins and to cleanse us from all unrighteousness" (1 John 1:9).

Recognition of sin in our life, whether recent or distant, should not produce a remorse one carries like a heavy burden. The exposure of sin should drive us to the Father who has given his Son to bear the judgment for sin on our behalf. There is forgiveness and cleansing in Christ. In 2 Corinthians 7:8-13, the apostle Paul speaks of the comfort that arises from grief producing repentance. Earlier in the same letter, he compelled the Corinthians to "forgive and comfort" the repentant brother, lest he "be overwhelmed by excessive sorrow" (2:7).

The apostle Paul was himself the "chief of sinners." An aggressive persecutor of the church, he was complicit in the death of people for their simple belief in Jesus (cf. Acts 7:58; 9:13-14). He imprisoned many on behalf of the Sanhedrin, yet he did not live burdened by guilt. He embraced the forgiveness offered in Jesus and moved forward in the joy of that forgiveness.

When Jesus has cleansed us, it is an affront to him to view ourselves as dirty. We were washed by the blood of the Lamb and should therefore freely and joyfully receive this marvelous gift he has given. To do otherwise is to call into question the efficacy of the Savior's sacrifice and the Father's promised forgiveness.

After we confess we must put the forgiven sin behind us—just as the Father places it as far as the east is from the west. Psalm 130 declares,

> If you, O LORD, should mark iniquities, O Lord, who could stand? But with you there is forgiveness, that you may be feared.
> **Psalm 130:3-4**

The Lord does not "mark" our sin. He erects no monument to our failure, to serve as a perpetual reminder. We must not build one to remind ourselves. Even if the person we wronged refuses to forgive or forget, we must not harbor our failure. Prodigals are skilled in using guilt to manipulate their parents (the inverse also occurs too often). It is painful when a child repeatedly throws in your face an episode from years ago that you have confessed and asked for forgiveness from someone. But you must understand such moments for what they are—a sinful attempt to manipulate you.

The point is this: once you confess, move on. Persistent and repeated confession of past sins will not move the heart of your prodigal. It also is an unbiblical response to sin. We confess. God forgives. He restores the joy of our relationship. This same pattern should guide our confession to others. A prodigal's failure to embrace restoration does not mean you should keep confessing your sin to him. Doing so will only empower him to justify his rebellion by blaming you.

RECOGNIZE THE LIMITS OF YOUR PARENTAL IMPACT

Your child was born with a sinful nature. You do not have the power to rectify this birth defect borne in all children from Cain onward. No amount of instruction or example can remove the stain of sin. It requires a work of the Spirit to bring a new birth. This is why Jesus said, "You must be born again" (John 3:7).

When told this truth, Nicodemus perceptively asked, "How

can a man be born when he is old? Can he enter a second time into his mother's womb and be born?" (John 3:4). Nicodemus was no fool; he was a teacher in Israel. He understood Jesus was not talking about physical birth. Nicodemus did not literally expect to be physically born again. Continuing the analogy Jesus began, he expressed his understanding that the task needed was impossible to accomplish himself. Jesus confirmed it was out of this Pharisee's control when he declared, "The wind blows where it wishes, and you hear its sound, but you do not know where it comes from or where it goes. So it is with everyone who is born of the Spirit" (v. 8).

The work of saving faith is a mystery in the hands of God and not dictated by the desires of men. As much as you might wish, you cannot control the response of your son or daughter to spiritual truth. We will return to this important reality in a later chapter.

Do Not Excuse Your Child's Actions

A parent will be tempted to excuse the choices of their prodigal in an effort to make up for their own deficiencies. This will have a negative influence on him, as excusing his conduct gives license to continue down a destructive path. Providing excuses for a prodigal's conduct to others also mislabels your offspring before those who can help. The body of Christ is the greatest resource apart from the direct work of the Spirit of God. We should yearn for fellow believers to rally around our wayward child with Christian love and a clear testimony of the truth. However, they cannot do so if we paint an inaccurate picture of our prodigal's condition.

Realize the Responsibility Borne by Your Prodigal

Your prodigal child is responsible for decisions he makes. Despite any failures on your part, he is accountable for his choices.

Though little spoken of in our day, God has made us with a conscience that serves as a reflection upon our thoughts and actions. Paul put it this way:

*For when Gentiles, who do not have the law, by nature
do what the law requires, they are a law to themselves,
even though they do not have the law. They show that
the work of the law is written on their hearts, while their
conscience also bears witness, and their conflicting
thoughts accuse or even excuse them.*
Romans 2:14–15

Nowhere in Scripture are the sins of men excused because someone else led them astray or failed to teach them aright. Those who lead others astray are accountable for their false leadership. Nevertheless, those who followed the sin of Korah experienced punishment just like the one who led them astray (Numbers 16:32). The Lord held them accountable for their choices—specifically, following the one who led them astray. No failure on your part excuses the sinful choices of your prodigal.

Loved ones of prodigals must embrace the same forgiveness that they pray their wayward family member will come to know. If we remain burdened with guilt, it may obscure the grace of God in our lives to our prodigal.

*In him we have redemption through his blood, the
forgiveness of our trespasses, according to the riches of
his grace*
Ephesians 1:7

4

Letting Them Bear Consequences

He had no bed to rest on at night, no closet or dresser for his clothes. No bathroom to take care of his personal hygiene. The temperature outside was dropping—he was cold, hungry, and homeless. In light of his circumstances, he did what he always did when in dire need. Our son called requesting we pay for a hotel room or an apartment for him. He was in the habit of turning any resources we provided into a means to obtain drugs. Since we lived hundreds of miles away, we could find no proof of his situation—or what he would actually do with any funds we provided. It was a difficult choice we faced many times. How much help do you give a prodigal? When do you allow him to bear the consequences of his destructive choices?

If a parent does not embrace the forgiveness God offers, it will be challenging to allow their prodigal to reap the consequences of his choices. When you live with the burden of guilt for your offspring's wayward path, it is difficult to draw appropriate lines to define where you will or will not offer help. Instead, in a mistaken effort to make up for your shortcomings, you will tend to give in to any request for help from your prodigal. Such responses will benefit no one.

What help should you provide a prodigal? Is there an unconditional ever-open door for him to live with you? Is he welcome at family gatherings? Should you cover the cost of housing? Do you provide a paid cell phone to assure contact when needed? Is it wise to pay for prescription medicines when illness strikes? What about providing food and clothing? There are no easy or straightforward answers to these questions. Just as circumstances change, so will the right response.

One of the most taxing parts of parenting a prodigal is the unending requests for help. Tension arises between spouses when they do not agree on how to respond to these requests. Couples who cannot agree on how to approach the prodigal in this area will find themselves in regular conflict. Rather than supporting one another through a difficult trial, they will be pitted against one another by a prodigal who learns how to drive a wedge between them (as well manipulate their conflict for his own purposes).

It is essential to recognize that while you may not agree on what should be done, you must come to an agreement on what will be done. Sometimes my wife and I were not of one mind regarding a specific request. In some cases, I yielded to her judgment, and we responded as she believed was best. On other occasions, I felt strongly about the matter, and we acted on the request in the manner I thought was best. In such instances, it is essential to respond in unity. Never let words such as "I don't agree with him, but your father says, no" spill from your lips. Do not seek favor with your prodigal by verbalizing your disagreement with your spouse. Simply declare, "We decided not to grant your request." Couples must never offer their prodigal a wedge to drive between them.

Agreeing on principles for decision-making is essential for the well-being of parents of prodigals. Married siblings of prodigals must also develop a unified approach. We found the following evaluation questions helpful in our journey with our prodigal:

Is it a True Need?

Scripture declares we should give to those in need. The parable of the Good Samaritan provides a poignant statement from our Lord on the expected response when one in need crosses our path (Luke 10:25-37). We are especially to meet the needs of those in our own household. The apostle Paul says, "if anyone does not provide for his relatives, and especially for members of his household, he has denied the faith and is worse than an unbeliever" (1 Timothy 5:8). These words are serious. If you fail to meet the needs of members of your family, you are worse than an unbeliever! Yet the Bible also says, "If anyone is not willing to work, let him not eat" (2 Thessalonians 3:10). There are times we should not give food to some who ask.

It is biblical to assess whether the request from your prodigal represents a true need. You have no obligation to sustain your prodigal at the level of comfort he once enjoyed as a part of your household. A car is not a necessity when public transportation is available. Clothes that are out of style or do not match will still keep him warm. Internet access is available through public libraries and need not be available in his apartment. A mattress on the floor will keep him every bit as comfortable as a regular bed.

Sometimes it is hard to make this assessment from a distance. When our son lived in Iowa while we lived in Indiana, it was difficult to evaluate his appeals for help. We struggled with the right response when he was without shelter or regular income. I spoke with a dear Christian friend from the police force in this town who provided assurance our son need never go hungry or freeze. There were sufficient places providing food and shelter to those in true need (more on such choices below).

There may also come a point when trust has been broken so many times that you decide there will be no further sharing of funds or other resources. You may come to the point where you want to declare, "We are done and will not provide you with any further help—ever." It is understandable when parents reach this point. We did ourselves. However, be cautious about declaring you will "never" help them or provide funds again. Things you cannot anticipate happening might change your mind. In addition, use of the word "never" may send a signal of a permanent termination of your relationship that you did not really intend. Even worse, it may reveal bitterness toward him has taken root in your heart.

Is There an Alternative Source for Help?

Sometimes prodigals seek help with areas of true need created by inappropriate spending choices. Your provision of help will enable those poor choices. When Paul declared in 2 Thessalonians 3:10 that one who does not work should not eat, he implied that working and sustaining themselves was an option for such individuals. To give them a handout when they had an alternative means to support themselves was a wrong choice.

Those with adult prodigals will struggle with whether to direct their offspring to available social services instead of meeting their needs yourself. Recall that the Bible says only those widows who have no opportunity for support from their family are to be placed on the widows list of the church (1 Timothy 5:3-8). Does this make it wrong for Christian parents not to support their adult children, having them turn to social services instead?

Faithful followers of Jesus may differ on this point. We live in a society that collects mandatory payments from citizens (taxes) that are used, in part, to create and sustain a social safety net for those in need. Access to these services most often requires an assessment of needs. I am unaware of any agencies that account for parental or sibling resources in assessing the need of an adult (or emancipated minor). In doing so, our society has recognized there is a point at which parental responsibility for ongoing support ends.[9] In our weekly work feeding the homeless, none of the volunteers my wife organizes have ever expressed resentment that family members of the homeless are not providing their needed food. We may not know why a homeless person is not receiving help from family, but we are glad to give a cup of cold water and a simple meal in Jesus' name. Those who see the destructive impact of many of our homeless clients quickly understand their estrangement from families and the place for others to help with basic needs.

The healthcare needs of a prodigal present a special problem. The lifestyle of such individuals puts them at risk for traumatic injuries, overdose, infections, and the consequences of uncontrolled chronic disease (such as diabetes). They use healthcare services more often than the average citizen does. What obligations do you have as a parent to meet the healthcare expenses of your adult prodigal? Should you pay their hospital and outpatient visit bills? Do you underwrite the cost of an insurance policy for them? Again, faithful followers of Jesus may conclude this issue

---

9   This is in contrast to the clear accounting of parental income when assessing financial aid for college (a non-essential), even into the early adult years.

differently. It is easy for someone who does not have a prodigal to quickly state, "Of course the parents should be responsible and not the tax payers!" However, you might draw a different conclusion if you were the one facing potential financial ruin from your adult offspring's healthcare bills.

In truth, only the very rich who choose to go without insurance pay their own way for healthcare. Even then, government grants and the philanthropy of others often subsidizes the facilities they use. The rest of us pay a fraction of the true costs because we are in shared risk pools, be they pools of employees, retirees, or active military personnel. Over the past two years, I consumed more healthcare than I paid for, out of pocket and through insurance premiums. Other university personnel consumed less than their personal contributions covered during this same period. I have consumed less than my monthly payments for insurance in other years. The point is this—almost none of us pay for our healthcare, others (especially employers) pay most of the costs. Those employers pass on the costs in the price set for their goods or services. The poor do not differ from the rest. The makeup of the shared risk pool is what varies. In addition, one means by which hospitals gain non-profit status (which is financially beneficial to them) is to agree to provide a certain amount of care for the indigent. In other words, built into their financial model is meeting the healthcare needs of the poor without reimbursement. For these reasons, I do not believe parents of prodigals should feel guilty about their offspring using resources established by our social safety net (1 Corinthians 4:3). I do not see this as a violation of the biblical admonition to care for those in one's own household.

Will Offering "Help" Impair Their Understanding of the Principle of Sowing and Reaping?

Bearing the consequences of one's choices can provide important moral instruction. Scripture reminds us, "God is not mocked, for whatever one sows, that will he also reap" (Galatians 6:7). Moreover, "the one who sows to his own flesh will from the flesh reap corruption" (v. 8). Reducing the natural consequences of sinful choices can blunt an important teaching mechanism designed by our Creator. The Lord has often used the brokenness arising from the weight of the consequences of destructive choices as the path to repentance for rebels. Our parental instincts will create within us a desire to protect our offspring from adversity, even into adulthood. To do so is unwise. Sympathize with his plight. Lament in the pain he is experiencing. But be careful about shielding him from the full consequences of the error of his ways.

When parenting, we create consequences for behavior to instruct our young children. A prodigal desperately needs instruction but is usually unwilling to receive it. Bearing the hard consequences of his destructive choices may be the most important instruction he receives. We must love him enough to watch him bear the painful consequences of his choices. Rest assured, no matter how estranged you have become from your prodigal, watching him bear the fruit of his choices will be hard. At the same time, reaping painful consequences from what he has sown may be the very means to seeing his heart change.

Can Help Be Misused?

While a parent may intend their dollars be used for paying the electric or water bill, they may find their prodigal redirecting the cash for unnecessary uses. Parents of prodigals learn through experience to pay bills directly rather than giving cash to their prodigal. Even then, one must think about the potential for an unapproved redirection of funds. Those with a prodigal involved in illicit drug use have probably learned the hard way the creativity of their offspring in turning help they provide into a means of getting drugs. Electronic items and clothing are sold, food is bartered for drugs or paraphernalia, and tuition gets reclaimed by dropping out of classes. Ad infinitum are the ways in which a prodigal will turn resources meant to help him into the means to get his substance of choice.

It is prudent to insist you will only provide help in such a way that he cannot not redirect those resources elsewhere. If you cannot assure resources will be used for the intended purpose, avoiding the requested help is probably the wise choice. But remember that God ultimately holds the individual receiving the funds accountable. When we try to love our prodigal with wisdom and decide to help, we need to surrender those resources we provide to the Lord—whether or not they end up used appropriately. It is really our Creator's resources the prodigal misuses, and it is to him prodigals owe the greatest accountability. This perspective will guard us against responding in anger if the funds end up being misdirected. Instances of misused funds should affect future help you may provide, but do not allow such instances to produce a festering anger within you.

DOES THE REQUEST PUT OTHERS AT RISK?

I presume most parents would be appalled by the option of choosing to allow your son to be homeless rather than take him into your home. Of course, most parents have not experienced a big SUV with tinted windows parked in front of their home, inhabited by a drug dealer to whom your son owes money. Most have not experienced a son who has destroyed walls in their home while under the influence of drugs. They have not had their mailbox used to exchange drugs in the middle of the night. Sadly, there came a time where my wife's safety became more important than my paternal care. Most parents only face such choices in their nightmares. For some, the nightmare becomes reality.

Parents of prodigals may find themselves in the position where providing help for their prodigal puts themselves or others they love at risk—physically, materially, or financially. I find no biblical support for a position that suggests you should jeopardize the physical safety of your family for the sake of a prodigal. Those with younger children at home need to consider these choices with special care. The impact of a prodigal's destructive choices within the home can be devastating. Younger siblings often look up to older ones and may be led astray if regularly under their influence.

I would have stood between my son and a bullet on any day. Nevertheless, I would also stand between my wife and my son in any way necessary to protect her from his destructive choices. I would also stand between him and my other children or their children to protect them. Fathers bear a special responsibility here. The protective love of a mother will be inclined to accept personal physical risk for her wayward child. The nurturing drive within them may be so strong that the better part of wisdom does not prevail. Men may need to fulfill their protective role by drawing lines others in the family find hard to accept. It would be wise to seek godly counsel before doing so to assure you are not overreacting. However, being the head of the household brings a special responsibility for the safety of your family. You cannot delegate this role to another.

Even more difficult to discern is the level of financial risk you should assume for the sake of your prodigal. We have known parents who were left holding the bag when their offspring jumped the bail their parents posted. Others have taken second mortgages to cover legal fees to assist their prodigal in minimizing the penalty for his illegal activity. Some co-signed car loans for vehicles soon totaled by their intoxicated offspring, putting themselves at personal liability for the injuries of others due to their co-ownership.

Dealing with requests to obligate yourself financially on behalf of your wayward child, sibling, or parent is probably inevitable. Thinking this through with care in advance is helpful. While the Bible is silent on this specific issue, it does warn us about making financial obligations we cannot keep. For example, Jesus painted as foolish one who would begin a construction project without first assuring he had resources to complete the task (Luke 14:28- 30). Scripture also warns about being a promissory for another. Proverbs 17:18 (NLT) declares, "It's poor judgment to guarantee another person's debt or put up security for a friend." Furthermore, "Don't agree to guarantee another person's debt or put up security for someone else. If you can't pay it, even your bed will be snatched from under you" (Proverbs 22:26-27 NLT). We are also told, "A man of great wrath will pay the penalty, for if you deliver him, you will only have to do it again" (Proverbs 19:19). Hence, I do not believe the Bible supports the notion of committing yourself to future financial obligations on behalf of your prodigal. They will seek to make you feel guilty for not doing so, but is it wise to put your obligations to your other family members at risk because of the destructive choices of a prodigal?

Does Helping Him Provide an Opportunity to Show Love?

When a prodigal reaches a point where you can no longer trust him in your home or provide resources you would normally share with your offspring, opportunities to show love are limited. Still, you want to keep the door open enough for him to see that a change in heart on his part can lead to restoration. You want to be there if the Lord begins to work on his heart. When your relationship has reached this point, words will not penetrate deeply. Acts of kindness will remind him of your love. Though others have abandoned him, you have not. You have placed clear boundaries but have not shut him out. In the parable of the prodigal son, the son obviously sensed enough of a crack in the door to return home.

When we lived in the same town as our son, we found giving rides to work or to medical appointments, while inconvenient for us, were regular opportunities to show love. If we could spare our son a walk that would normally take one hour by giving him a lift, we did so. Yes, we could have declined and said this was just part of the price he was paying for his destructive choices. However, it was an opportunity to remind him that we loved him enough to inconvenience ourselves for his good. Doing something for someone who often misused us was also a healthy blow to our pride. The Lord can use something as simple as personal inconvenience to refine us.

Besides questions about providing tangible help when asked, parents and siblings of prodigals will face questions about sharing gifts within a family at occasions such as birthdays and Christmas. These occasions can be a time to keep the lines of communication open. After ten years of work with the homeless in our town, we have found the atmosphere in our local shelter to be markedly glum during the holidays—especially Christmas and Thanksgiving. Even when you have minimal-to-no contact with your prodigal, such occasions in the calendar provide an opportunity to remind him you have not forgotten him. It serves as a regular reminder that you will be there should he turn from his destructive path.

Providing practical help to meet a real need is one way to direct gifts on special occasions like birthdays. As mentioned earlier, those with prodigals who abuse chemical substances will find a special challenge doing so in a way that doesn't provide resources for drugs. Parents may also struggle with a sense of inequality in the way they treat their other children compared to the prodigal— for example, the amount of money they spend on gifts for each. Yet the simple reality is their children are not the same and no reasonable person would expect you to treat them as though they were. The prodigal has chosen a path that, in essence, has rejected the core of who you are as a person. He should have no expectation you would treat him like your other children who have not chosen to reject the path on which you led them.

Deciding how to deal with a prodigal in your will is both necessary and difficult. You must consider the potential consequences of leaving a significant amount of cash to one involved in a destructive lifestyle. As stewards of the resources God has given, parents need to be wise about how these resources are dispersed upon their death. You also don't want to leave your other children to deal with the fruit of what may be seen as an inequitable distribution of resources. In particular, you don't want to leave one of them to deal with the incessant badgering for funds from a prodigal sibling. It is wise to consult an estate attorney to guide you through options to be good stewards of all God has given you.

Refusing requests to help your prodigal will be painful. He will repeatedly push you to give in and threaten you with all kinds of stories of what will happen if you do not meet his demands. Giving in will be the simplest thing to do, but it will also help him continue on his destructive path.

Do not be deceived: God is not mocked, for whatever one sows, that will he also reap.
Galatians 6:7

5

FACING THE HARD REALITY

"Didn't he ever make a profession of faith in Christ as a child?" This question came in response to a request to pray for our wayward son—in particular, asking God to show mercy and save his soul. Since our son grew up in the church, the questioner assumed he experienced many opportunities as a young boy to hear the gospel. Surely, they thought, he responded to an invitation at some point as a young child. Unfortunately, he gave no evidence of a relationship with Jesus in his teenage or adult life.

I could not count the number of times we heard parents make statements about their children such as, "I take comfort from the fact that he made a profession of faith when he was five, so I know he is saved. But he has not walked with the Lord for three decades." We have often conversed with parents whose offspring gives no present evidence of saving faith, yet they treat their grown child as though he were eternally secure, just temporarily estranged from God.

It is easy, though unhealthy, for a parent to cling to a false hope regarding their child's eternal state. No parent wants to face the hard truth that the sudden earthly departure of his or her child will lead to eternal punishment. But if we do not face the hard reality of our child's apparent eternal state, we will err in the manner that we pray to God and in the manner we speak to our child. An individual who needs the mercy of God to draw him into the Father's forever family needs to be prayed for, and spoken to, differently than one who is a believer that has fallen into sin. If we do not determine the true spiritual state of our children to the best of our ability, our approach to them will not address their true need.

A Proper Place for Discernment

Judging the spiritual state of another person is challenging and controversial. To question the professed confession of another is often seen as a threat to the marvelous truth of eternal security. But if parents of prodigals do not diagnose the condition of their children's hearts, they will not fulfill their parental responsibility. Sometimes even the most careful discernment leaves us with uncertainty. As true as this may be, over the years I have conversed with many a parent whose description of their child's life should leave no confusion as to his eternal state. Yet they cling to the notion of their offspring's eternal security despite all evidence to the contrary.

Jesus spoke with clarity about whether an individual belongs to him, the eternal life-giving vine:

> *For no good tree bears bad fruit, nor again does a bad tree bear good fruit, for each tree is known by its own fruit.*
> **Luke 6:43–44a**

It is clear from his words that fruit, visible evidence manifesting itself externally, is produced where saving faith resides. How can it be otherwise? The Bible declares that before salvation we "were dead in trespasses and sins" (Ephesians 2:1). Not dull, but dead! There is no evidence of spiritual life in those who are spiritually dead.

> *But God, being rich in mercy, because of the great love with which he loved us, even when we were dead in our trespasses, made us alive together with Christ.*
> **Ephesians 2:4–5a**

The new birth of which Christ spoke brings true life—spiritual life. Believers have "passed out of death into life" (1 John 3:14). Where life exists, there will be evidence of this life. If we came across a man lying in a street, we would seek evidence of life remaining within—heartbeat, respiration, responsiveness to pain, or other physical signs that he is alive. If we found no evidence of life, we would administer CPR. In like manner, where spiritual life resides there is discernible evidence of this life. If one claims spiritual life, but provides no evidence, we rightly view the claim as false. As simply spoken in the Bible, "faith by itself, if it does not have works, is dead" (James 2:17). Works are not the path to salvation, but works are the expected fruit of salvation.

Others have, with greater eloquence and depth, discussed the inevitability of fruit where new life in the Spirit exists.[10] A changed life is the expected manifestation of salvation. Moreover, the clearest evidence of the truthfulness of one's profession is perseverance. John declared,

> by this we know that we have come to know him, if we
> keep his commandments. Whoever says "I know him"
> but does not keep his commandments is a liar, and the
> truth is not in him.
> **1 John 2:3–4a**

Salvation is an event occurring in a moment of time. But this miraculous event does not leave us as we were before salvation. Where salvation has occurred, there will inevitably be a life given to obedience to the commands of Christ, not in perfection, but in pattern. There is no biblical basis to conclude an individual living for years in open rebellion against the commands of Christ is a believer. The apostle John made this plain when he declared,

> No one born of God makes a practice of sinning, for
> God's seed abides in him, and he cannot keep on sinning
> because he has been born of God. By this it is evident
> who are the children of God, and who are the children of
> the devil: whoever does not practice righteousness is not
> of God
> **1 John 3:9–10**

Perhaps the clearest evidence of the Christian life is the ex-

---

10   For example, see A.W. Tozer, *I Call It Heresy!*, (Camp Hill, Pa.: Christian Publications, 1991) and John F. MacArthur, *The Gospel According to Jesus: What Is Authentic Faith?*, Revised and Expanded Anniversary Edition, (Grand Rapids, Mi.: Zondervan, 2008).

pressed sense that Christ is precious to them. Jesus said, "If God were your Father, you would love me" (John 8:42). Writing to believers, Peter characterized them by saying, "Though you have not seen him, you love him" (1 Peter 1:8). In his final intimate moment with the apostle Peter, Jesus did not ask whether Peter believed this or that. Instead, he asked, "Do you love me?"(John 21:15-17). Loving Jesus is the clearest evidence of true belief. An absence of such love yields condemnation—"If anyone has no love for the Lord, let him be accursed" (1 Corinthians 16:22). Saving faith is more than just *believing something*, it is *loving someone*. Specifically, loving the Lord Jesus.

Does your child, sibling, spouse, or parent give evidence that Jesus is precious to him? Can you sense an affection for Jesus? Does he spend time with Jesus, in the Word and prayer? Does he wish to talk about the Lord? Has he been willing to make sacrifices of time, treasure, or talent because of his love for Jesus? If there is no evidence the Lord is precious to him, then there is no basis to conclude that he belongs to Christ.

A DISCOMFORTING REALITY

Scripture is abundantly clear that not all who profess faith in Christ are believers. Consider the words of Jesus himself:

> *Not everyone who says to me, "Lord, Lord," will enter the kingdom of heaven, but the one who does the will of my Father who is in heaven.*
> **Matthew 7:21**

You may not be comfortable with this truth, but they are the plain words of Jesus. People will falsely label themselves as Christians. Moreover, the Lord Jesus indicated that abiding or enduring is the valid measure of one's profession:

> *So Jesus said to the Jews who had believed in him, "If you abide in my word, you are truly my disciples, and you will know the truth, and the truth will set you free."*
> **John 8:31-32**

The individuals who Jesus addressed "had believed in him." They gave assent to his teaching. There was some level of agreement that he was who he claimed to be. But to be shown to be "truly my disciples," they would abide in his word. Persevering in the belief they claimed would be the measuring rod to show they were true disciples. Paul speaks of those who "profess to know God, but deny him by their works" (Titus 1:16). There are those with lying lips, people whose deeds show their profession to be false.

Because of this truth, it is not wrong to question the eternal condition of one who lives contrary to a profession made many years ago as a child (or even as an adult). Jesus declared, "each tree is known by its own fruit" (Luke 6:44a). This is why Paul challenged the Corinthians,

> *Examine yourselves, to see whether you are in the faith. Test yourselves. Or do you not realize this about yourselves, that Jesus Christ is in you?—unless indeed you fail to meet the test!*
> **2 Corinthians 13:5**

Some parents acknowledge this truth, but understandably find it hard to apply to their own son, daughter, or other loved one—even when their prodigal verbally renounces Christ. It is heart-wrenching to face this hard truth. The desire of their heart blocks their mind from going in such a direction. After our son's death, several individuals—in person and in writing—strongly (and I mean strongly) rebuked us for speaking of our son as having died without Christ. Some seemed truly angered by our expression of this view. They admonished us to have faith that God saved him before his last breath, as though by saying this with confidence would make it so.

It is likely there will be readers who find themselves discomforted by the foregoing discussion—for this topic is among the hard truths of Scripture. Others will object because of the personal experience of a prodigal who has returned. God has graciously grabbed his heart, and he returned expressing a desire to rededicate his life to Christ. He sees himself not as newly born again, but rather returning to the Lord he foolishly abandoned for a period. What are we to conclude from these experiences? I have known such individuals over the years. Often, as they mature in their faith, they look back and conclude they were not saved as a young person. Rather, the true point of salvation was upon their "return."

Sometimes we allow experience to be the filter through which we interpret Scripture. In doing so, we reverse the correct approach. I saw this while teaching pastors and other church leaders in Russia in the mid-1990s. When persecution of Christians arose in the former Soviet Union, many who previously professed faith walked away. Things changed when churches rebuilt during the new openness under Mikhail Gorbachev. Some who previously walked away repented at evangelistic meetings and desired to return. Our brothers in church leadership in Russia interpreted this experience as evidence one could lose their salvation. This caused them to interpret certain passages in Scripture (such as the warning passages in Hebrews) to support their experientially driven notion that you could lose your salvation. They failed to see Scripture teaches the reality that there will be those who falsely profess faith in Christ and then fall away (see chapter 7).

As Martyn Lloyd-Jones wisely said, "We should not interpret Scripture in the light of our experiences, but we should examine our experiences in the light of the teaching of the Scripture."[11] I am not wise enough to understand the full spectrum of human experience; I presume none of us would claim to be. Only the Lord knows the heart. Yet, where in Scripture is there support for the notion that a "Christian" can live in persistent rebellion for years with no evidence of saving faith? What support is there of the Spirit indwelling someone, as he does all true believers, with no evidence of his presence? In contrast, we have considered several passages in Scripture telling us such individuals are not true believers—they are false.

There is a significant difference between an individual who professes faith in Christ, and then at some point surrenders to a particular sin, versus one who once professed faith but now lives

---

11   Martyn Lloyd-Jones, *Joy Unspeakable: Power & Revival in the Holy Spirit*, (Chicago, Ill.: Harold Shaw Publishers, 1984), p. 16-17.

in full-bore rebellion. First Corinthians 5 introduces us to a man fitting the first description. A man among the Corinthians was doing the unthinkable—living in sin with his father's wife. Note this man had not walked away from the faith. He is spoken of as being "among you" (v. 1). He remained in the fellowship and did not reject the faith. But he was in grievous sin. Importantly, when confronted with his sin, he repented (2 Corinthians 2). Such is the pattern of a true believer who falls into sin. When confronted by the church, they repent. This differs from one who openly rejects the faith they once professed and now lives devoid of evidence of the Spirit within. In the latter case, Scripture would point to such an individual as a false professor.

It is an errant theology that neutralizes the repeated threats of judgment in Scripture upon those who surrender themselves to sin. True believers do not make peace with sin in their lives (cf. Matthew 5:29 and 1 Peter 2:11). They fight it. They wage war against it. Yes, followers of Jesus may lose some battles. At times, they do so with painful frequency. But they do not hoist up a white flag and declare, "I am yours and will do your bidding." Those who have surrendered to the passion of the flesh are destined for judgment and not for heaven (cf. Colossians 3:5-6).

This is one of the hard truths many find difficult to embrace. Nevertheless, ignoring a hard reality will not make it less real. If we are going to help our wayward child or loved one, we must begin with an accurate diagnosis of the condition of his heart. As in clinical medicine, a misdiagnosis can result in a treatment that does more harm than good. Would we want to give someone a false sense of security as to the state of his soul?

WHEN A PARENT JUDGES WELL

Charles Haddon Spurgeon gives testimony to the impact of a mother who, with keen insight, diagnosed the condition of the hearts of her children:

> Yet I cannot tell how much I owe to the solemn words of my good mother. It was the custom, on Sunday evenings, while we were yet little children, for her to stay at home with us,

and then we sat round the table, and read verse by verse, and she explained the Scripture to us. After that was done, then came the time of pleading; there was a little piece of *Alleine's Alarm*, or of Baxter's *Call to the Unconverted*, and this was read with pointed observations made to each of us as we sat round the table; and the question was asked, how long it would be before we would think about our state, how long before we would seek the Lord. Then came a mother's prayer, and some of the words of that prayer we shall never forget, even when our hair is grey. I remember, on one occasion, her praying thus: "Now, Lord, if my children go on in their sins, it will not be from ignorance that they perish, and my soul must bear a swift witness against them at the day of judgment if they lay not hold of Christ." That thought of a mother's bearing swift witness against me, pierced my conscience, and stirred my heart.[12]

To provide spiritual aid to our prodigal, we must see his heart rightly. Many people made some outward gesture as a young child that they or their parents hold on to as their parachute to safety when the end comes—although their lives are on a persistent destructive downward path. Exposing the true nature of their heart is the first step off that perilous road.

CONFRONTING THE PRODIGAL

How do we confront one who has turned off the godly path on which we tried to lead them? It first requires discerning what they actually believe—what is the source of their hope in life, if any? Where does it deviate from the truth of Scripture? Do they see themselves as a sinner before God? The apostle Paul could strategically confront the Athenians because he first sought to understand what they believed (Acts 17:22-31). Jesus, who certainly saw into the heart of people in ways we cannot, confronted the rich young ruler in the exact spot where idolatry ruled his heart (Luke 18:22). We will never know what our children believe if we do not ask.

---

12   Charles H. Spurgeon, *Early Religious Impressions*, https://www.spurgeon.org/resource-library/books/ix-early-religious-impressions#flipbook/3

Admittedly, a prodigal may not be willing to open their heart to a parent from whom they have rebelled. They know what you believe and where you will take the conversation. Consequently, they may avoid like the plague any discussion of spiritual things. They may be unwilling to reveal what is in their hearts. Herein lies one of the joys of being a part of the body of Christ. If raised in the church, there are likely some for whom they hold respect or affection. It may even be their peers in the church. Recruit their help if you can. Some prodigals will open up to a sibling or more distant family member. Don't underestimate the ability of a grandparent to influence their lives. Just as you call upon the God of heaven to intervene in their lives, be vulnerable enough to draw members of the body into the pursuit of your prodigal.

We must remember it is not about lifestyle when confronting a prodigal, even regarding issues that unnerve us. We may not appreciate the tattoos or piercings adorning their body, but these things are of no eternal significance. Don't focus on them as though they were. They may be making many unwise choices, yet these are not the heart of the matter. We must draw them to the person of Jesus. We must point them to who he is, why he came, what he has done, and why we all so desperately need the salvation he offers.

There are many who give the advice to "just love them and let God work on their heart." It is good and right to show love in terms of acts of kindness. Tolerating unwise, but non-essential, choices is advisable in your relationship with a prodigal. Nevertheless, none of these things will bring them to saving faith. We may wish for them to have their very own Damascus-road experience. But Scripture and history both indicate it is the communication of the Word of God through people that will be used to bring them to repentance leading to salvation (Romans 10:14-15). We must lay the word before them whenever possible. We should do so wisely and lovingly. The time and place is often as important as the manner. Our efforts should be bathed in prayer. But the sword of the Spirit is the instrument needed, and we should not be afraid to wield it.

In bringing the Word of God to bear on your prodigal, be certain not to do so in anger. The Word of God is likened to a sword, not a sledgehammer. It is properly used with surgical precision—not as an instrument with which to bludgeon them. We can all recall examples when someone used the Word to condemn rather than convict or enlighten. Such errant applications of proclaiming the Word should not cause us to avoid its use with our prodigal.

The Nature of the Battle

Loved ones of prodigals must realize the battle for the soul of their wayward child, sibling, spouse, or parent is not intellectual. It is spiritual. Our struggle is not "against flesh and blood, but against the rulers, against the authorities, against the cosmic powers over this present darkness, against the spiritual forces of evil in the heavenly places" (Ephesians 6:12). This battle, to which Paul refers, is not out there somewhere; it is in your family, and fought over the soul of your loved one. The prince of this world seeks to capture the souls of men. Songwriters Lauren Daigle and Michael Farren have succinctly expressed the state of prodigals: "the enemy has whispered lies and led them off as slaves."[13] The prophet Isaiah characterizes this enemy as the one "who did not let his prisoners go home" (14:17). Reading those words from Isaiah should make us shudder. Our enemy is formidable. His grip on them will not be loosened by intellectual arguments or simple acts of kindness. It will require a work of the Spirit of God to open their eyes to their perilous state. We must plead for the Lord to do so and appeal to others to join us in this supplication.

Those who have surrendered to reckless living must come to see that they stand as condemned before God—not condemned before you, but before God. Just like every other person born into this world. No one cries out for rescue without first recognizing his or her desperate state.

Repent, therefore, of this wickedness of yours ... For I see that you are in the gall of bitterness and in the bond of iniquity.
Acts 8:22a, 23

---

13 Come Alive lyrics © Warner/Chappell Music, Inc, Capitol Christian Music Group

6

UNDERSTANDING WHY

The bride was beautiful. The groom, an answer to our prayers. Both loved Jesus, loved one another, and were serving him in a local church near the university they attended. Years of prayers were answered the day I gave our daughter away to the one to whom she would cleave, Josh. The day should have been a time of pure joy. Disappointingly, there was underlying tension. Our son's presence kept us on edge. Would he try to steal from a guest? What if he slipped out to use drugs? Could he do something unmercifully embarrassing to his older sister? How do we make him feel welcome—yet keep an eye on him?

While none of our fears unfolded, reflecting on this day was a study in contrasts. Being close in age, the life experience of these two siblings had so much in common. Why had their paths diverged so sharply? Why had one surrendered to Christ at a young age while the other presumably lived in rebellion to his last day?

Parents of a prodigal are inclined to struggle with the question of why. Why does a child become a prodigal? Why do they turn away from us and the God we serve? It is especially inexplicable when other children from the same family are walking in the faith. I have heard many parents and a few authors seek to answer such questions for specific prodigals. Some blame atheistic professors who undermined their child's faith. Others blame a bad choice of friends. More will blame an absent father or a doting mother. Still others blame the genes passed on from their ancestors.

Augustine of Hippo, himself a prodigal, wrote from personal experience when he said, "It is not reason that turns the young man from God, it is the flesh. Skepticism but provides him with the excuses for the new life he is leading."[14] In essence, Augustine is saying that those who give themselves over to ruinous living do not do so because they have nothing to believe. They do so because they have become a slave to their flesh. The flesh, not the intellect, has driven them astray.

Augustine is close, but perhaps misstates rebellion's true point of origin. In reality, the prodigal does not turn from God. He never turned to God in the first place. A prodigal has done what comes naturally. He may have pretended for a period of time, but eventually, his outward life reveals the true nature of his heart. Augustine showed this in his own life choices. This truth is also evident in the life of Cain. Yet to understand the why behind the choices of the prodigal, one must go back to the first rebellion.

THE ROOT OF ALL REBELLION

Mystery shrouds the nature of God's creation of the angelic host. In his sovereign wisdom, God withholds these details from his earthbound creatures. Nevertheless, the Lord Jesus testified of the existence of the angelic host and their ongoing impact on God's creation. Though people debate the timing, serious students of the Bible acknowledge a rebellion occurred among the angelic host. Perhaps as many as one third of these angelic beings turned from their Creator (Revelation 12:4).

Think of this. Myriads of beings living in the presence of their glorious Creator exercised their freedom of choice to turn away from him. Is it a stretch to say these are the first prodigals in all of eternity? Do you think God understands the pain of the parent of a prodigal? He knows it deeply. Unlike earthly parents of prodigals, there was no shortcoming on his part. Despite this, they turned from his way. God did not spare himself this painful experience. Why should Christian parents expect to be spared?

The prodigals of heaven are just the beginning of a cascade of prodigals continuing on earth to this day. As Adam and Eve dwelt in the garden, they encountered a beautiful creature. His beguiling beauty hid his evil intent. He led them to question the

14   Quoted in Ruth Bell Graham, *Prodigals and Those Who Love Them*, (Grand Rapids, Mi.: Baker Books, 1999), 21.

veracity of God's word. They took the bait and bit the forbidden fruit. With this simple act, the pristine creation of humanity fell into a death spiral. The physical world in which they dwelt altered beyond their full comprehension. Things would never be the same again.

Importantly, Adam and Eve's choice had an impact beyond their immediate experience. The stain of sin was passed to their offspring and all offspring born of man from then on. Adam and Eve bore a greater burden than any parent of a prodigal today. In truth, Cain's rebellion was the direct fruit of their action. God created and placed them into the sinless environment of the garden of Eden. Theirs was the joy of communing with God without hindrance. Yet they chose to disobey. Their disobedience brought the contamination of sin into every aspect of the world of humanity and passed it on to every generation after them. The apostle Paul tells us "sin came into the world through one man" (Romans 5:12). He further explains, "in Adam all die." Adam and Eve saw the fruit of their fateful choice through the rebellion of their son Cain and the consequent death of their son Abel. We see the continued fruit of their choice throughout the sad history of humanity.

David understood the inheritable nature of sin when he said, "I was brought forth in iniquity and in sin did my mother conceive me" (Psalm 51:5). This inheritable nature of sin necessitated Jesus to be born of woman but not of a man. His conception by the Holy Spirit to a virgin was the only means by which the Messiah could enter this world without a sinful nature (Luke 1:35). His sinless nature was essential if he was to be the spotless Lamb of God sacrificed for us.

THE FRUIT OF THE FALL

The message is this: from Cain onward, prodigals have simply done what comes naturally. All are born with a sinful nature, "for all have sinned and fall short of the glory of God" (Romans 3:23). Indeed, "None is righteous, no, not one; no one understands, no one seeks for God" (Romans 3:10-11).

Men and women choose a path apart from God and surrender to their flesh because they are born with a sinful nature. All will take this path apart from a miraculous and gracious work of the Spirit of God. All. Everyone. Apart from the grace of God, the path of the prodigal would be the journey of everyone. However difficult it may be for parents to think of their offspring as stained through and through with sin, the Bible declares it so. The Psalmist says, "The wicked are estranged from the womb; they go astray from birth" (Psalm 58:3).

It is not the choice of the prodigal that should be beyond our understanding but the choice of the one who surrenders their life to Christ. This is the path exceeding human understanding and is a work as mysterious as the origin of the wind (John 3:8).

Our current society tries to provide biological or environmental explanations for all forms of aberrant behavior. In addition, we increasingly see efforts to redefine the boundaries of acceptable behavior. Moral choices once universally seen as wrong are now being presented as alternative lifestyles to be celebrated. Like the proverbial frog in the pool of slowly increasing water temperature, the thinking of many Christians is slowly distorted by the biological determinism of our age—manifested by its incessant efforts to remove moral judgement from the equation. The slow burn of moral decay seems indiscernible to many. Parents and other loved ones of prodigals are tempted to embrace the spirit of the age and view their prodigal's conduct as something other than the natural outgrowth of a fallen humanity because the truth is painful. Yet denying or ignoring the truth does not lead us to a better place. It never has, and it never will.

THE POWER OF THE EVIL ONE

There are individuals with diseases of the brain that affect their behavior, and there also may be environmental factors that influence their actions. But Scripture is clear regarding the power of the fallen flesh. Besides the flesh, the Bible declares there is an enemy who often captures the hearts of men. Not just generally, but specifically. The apostle Paul instructs Timothy to correct his opponents so "they may escape the snare of the devil, after being captured by him to do his will" (2 Timothy 2:26). Since they were captured, they must have been previously free from his grip. Something happened to place them into his captivity. Scripture indicates this was true of the first prodigal born on the earth:

We should not be like Cain, who was of the evil one and
murdered his brother.
1 John 3:12

Cain was not just a misguided soul. He was not merely led by the flesh. The serpent who beguiled his parents captured his heart, and as a result, he murdered his brother. Consider what is said of Judas, the prodigal who betrayed Jesus:

So when he had dipped the morsel, he gave it to Judas,
the son of Simon Iscariot. Then after he had taken the
morsel, Satan entered into him. Jesus said to him, "What
you are going to do, do quickly."
John 13:26b-27

Satan led Judas to carry out the betrayal of Jesus—not in a general sense, but specifically entering into the soul of this disciple of Jesus. This book will not address the difference between belonging to the kingdom of darkness in a broad sense and being a tool of Satan in particular. But Scripture points to some who appear to be particularly captured and used for Satan's evil ends. In these individuals, we especially see depths of evil. To them a special warning is given:

Woe to them! For they walked in the way of Cain and
abandoned themselves for the sake of gain to Balaam's
error and perished in Korah's rebellion.
Jude 11

THE DARKENING OF FUTILE HEARTS

It is also true that while all those without Christ are headed to perdition, not all surrender completely to the flesh. In other words, not all people are as evil as they could be. Many lost people do not abuse those around them or degrade themselves by fully surrendering to every passion of their flesh. This leaves the parent of a prodigal wondering why their child has surrendered themselves to degrading passions, while other lost souls display a modicum of propriety. Many of our friends' sons and daughters have not spent time in prison nor are they addicted to drugs even though they are lost. They have not morphed into unrecognizable people. Why do others spiral so deeply down into the cesspool of sin?

Society and social norms place a measure of restraint on many people. Whether it is their inner conscience or an unwillingness to experience the loss they might incur by violating those restraints, some individuals are inhibited from fully surrendering to their inner sinful desires. Others arrive at a point where such external restraints are meaningless. Like Pharaoh at the time of Moses, they have hardened their hearts and no longer hear the voice of restraint.

Frighteningly, God has surrendered some individuals over to the full measure of the destructive path they have chosen. They crossed a line and the Lord then removes restraining influences. Romans 1 declares that some "became futile in their thinking, and their futile hearts were darkened" (Romans 1:21). Light has been removed. They have come to a point where they can no longer see what they once had the opportunity to see. Because they turned from him, "God gave them up in the lusts of their hearts to impurity, to the dishonoring of their bodies among themselves, because they exchanged the truth about God for a lie and worshiped and served the creature rather than the Creator" (vv. 24-25). For some, the full downward spiral into the depths of sin is a manifestation of the judgment of God. A troubling truth to hear. Nevertheless, it is a truth plainly declared in the Word of God.

Why do offspring become prodigals? Because this is the natural path of fallen humanity. The true mystery lies not in the destructive choice of the prodigal, but in the choice of the one who turns from sin and embraces Christ. Therein lies a glorious mystery!

*The wind blows where it wishes, and you hear its sound,
but you do not know where it comes from or where it
goes. So it is with everyone who is born of the Spirit.*
John 3:8

7

Dealing with False Professions

Within the first hour of our return drive, we realized the person in the back seat was not who we expected. Like parents to whom a hospital had inadvertently given the wrong baby, a sense of panic grew within us. We drove six hours the night before to pick him up. Our discussion during this evening drive centered on our hopes for a new beginning. For three years, we corresponded by mail and occasional telephone calls. He was, we believed, one we could warmly welcome into our home. His testimony gave evidence he had become a sincere follower of Jesus. When he prayed over the phone, his words melted our hearts. With both relief and excitement, we thought this testimony was the answer to years of fervent prayer. Yet now, just one hour into our journey together, we had a growing suspicion he had played us for fools.

It began with a phone call from our son in prison. He declared that being in the belly of a maximum-security prison forced him to realize the desperate state of his life. He was done with trying to run his own life and had surrendered to Christ. We were, at first, skeptical. We heard similar lines from him before. Over time, this seemed different. His letters suggested he was seeing things for the first time with spiritual eyes. He asked about doing a Bible study together, which he did with me by correspondence. We began in 1 John. His answers to the questions were perceptive, suggesting a changed heart. Now, at the beginning of our phone calls, he asked us to pray so that we would not run out of time to do so. He often asked to pray himself, and his words warmed our hearts. We started to believe God had answered our many years of prayer and had visited our son with saving grace.

Not long after beginning this long-distance communication with him in prison, he spoke about what he would do when he was released. He seemed excited about the opportunity when we spoke to him about a residential ministry providing discipleship and training in the culinary arts. He frequently expressed a desire to be a chef and often found work as a cook in various restaurants. After we sent him some literature, he excitedly declared that he wanted to enter into this ministry's multi-year program. We saw a glimmer of light. Perhaps there was an exit from the dark tunnel through which he had been traveling for the past decade. As the time neared for his release, he raised doubts about his readiness to enter the aforementioned program immediately after leaving prison. These were legitimate concerns; we discussed each with care.

He soon broached the subject of living with us for a period of transition. He thought this would enable him to receive biblical counseling and discipleship from our church. We were hesitant at first, but we also could see some rationale for bringing him into our home before entering a long-term program. We read books on prisoner reentry and established an infrastructure of discipleship, counseling, and accountability—even creating a contract for him to sign. He readily agreed he would do all these things. Still, there were a few persistent warning flags. We struggled with knowing whether we were expecting too much from him. How much change should we expect from someone whose life had been on a downward destructive spiral for years? How can you assess the heart of someone so far away in a maximum security prison? What evidence of change can they provide?

When we picked him up from prison, he boasted of all the things he got away with while incarcerated. He deflected any spiritual questions during the drive, choosing instead mundane topics, seemingly intent on impressing us with his ingenuity in working the prison system to his advantage. He joked about the antics of fellow prisoners and the thickheadedness of the guards.

Within two weeks, the truth was undeniable. He cunningly played us, knowing what we hoped to hear and how he could position himself to live in our home.

Some parents of prodigals have walked the hard road of a false profession of faith by their son or daughter—only to be heartbroken, realizing it was a manipulative effort to gain some advantage from them. Having grown up in a Christian home, prodigals are well versed in what to say and do to give their parents hope that their profession may be real. Not wanting to thwart the work of the Spirit, and excited to think their prayers have been answered, parents may take the profession at face value and welcome their prodigal home. Soon, the reality brings disappointment and the deep pain of betrayal. We have watched spouses and siblings of prodigals walk through this same distressing experience.

Two issues arise with such experiences. First, how do you respond to a profession of faith from your prodigal? Second, how do you live with the deep disappointment of a false profession?

RESPONDING TO A PRODIGAL'S PROFESSION OF FAITH

It is understandable when loved ones jump at the first sign of spiritual life in their prodigal. The slightest sign the Spirit of God has quickened their hearts enlivens hope in those who love them. Nevertheless, with his incomparable insight, the Lord Jesus commends a realistic approach through his parable of the sower and the soils.

> *And he told them many things in parables, saying: "A sower went out to sow. And as he sowed, some seeds fell along the path, and the birds came and devoured them. Other seeds fell on rocky ground, where they did not have much soil, and immediately they sprang up, since they had no depth of soil, but when the sun rose they were scorched. And since they had no root, they withered away. Other seeds fell among thorns, and the thorns grew up and choked them. Other seeds fell on good soil and produced grain, some a hundredfold, some sixty, some thirty. He who has ears, let him hear."*
> **Matthew 13:3-9**

Jesus then provides the meaning of this important parable:

> *Hear then the parable of the sower: When anyone hears the word of the kingdom and does not understand it, the evil one comes and snatches away what has been sown in his heart. This is what was sown along the path. As for what was sown on rocky ground, this is the one who hears the word and immediately receives it with joy, yet he has no root in himself, but endures for a while, and when tribulation or persecution arises on account of the word, immediately he falls away. As for what was sown among thorns, this is the one who hears the word, but the cares of the world and the deceitfulness of riches choke the word, and it proves unfruitful. As for what was sown on good soil, this is the one who hears the word and understands it. He indeed bears fruit and yields, in one case a hundredfold, in another sixty, and in another thirty.*
>
> **Matthew 13:18-23**

The Lord Jesus portrays multiple responses to the Word of God, the means the Father uses to draw sinners to himself. In some, it is as if the Word fell on stony soil—it does not penetrate the surface. For others, there is a momentary expression of joy in response to the Word, but there is no root. As soon as trials or tribulations arise, they fall away. Others who receive the word give an initial response, only to give way to the cares of the world and the lusts of the flesh. Only the last, those who bear fruit over time, represent true salvation.[15]

This parable tells us we should regard with realism any profession of faith. Proverbs 14:15 points out that "[t]he simple believes everything, but the prudent gives thought to his steps." Simply put, faith professed should not be trusted until it is tested, even by the one making the profession.[16] Only time and trials will enable us to discern if the profession reflects genuine saving faith.

---

15   For a deeper discussion of this parable, see chapter 2 in John F. MacArthur, *Parables—The Mysteries of God's Kingdom Revealed Through the Stories Jesus Told*, (Nashville, Tn.: Thomas Nelson, 2015).

16   J. I. Packer describes this clearly articulated perspective of the Puritan writers in his discussion of their view on assurance in his helpful book—*A Quest for Godliness: The Puritan Vision of the Christian Life*, (Wheaton, Ill.: Crossway, 1990). This sentence is a rewording of Packer's summary of this perspective on page 182.

Does this mean we should treat those professing faith with skepticism? The Bible would not support such an approach. When John the Baptist called people to repent and be baptized, there is no evidence he waited for a period of testing to bring them into the waters of baptism. When the crowds responded to Peter's first sermon with the appeal, "Brothers, what shall we do?" that very day they were baptized and welcomed into the church upon their declaration of repentance (Acts 2:37-41). A similar pattern occurs throughout the book of Acts.

The pattern in Scripture commends accepting a profession at face value, embracing the one making the profession into Christian fellowship. Like all church members, this should include discipleship and accountability. If evidence accumulates raising questions about the faith of an individual, admonish them as a member of the family. When a pattern of sin from which they do not immediately repent arises, Matthew 18 outlines a pattern of discipline. If the person remains unresponsive to the appeal of the body of Christ, they are to be put out of the church (Matthew 18:15-17). Sometimes, this departure reveals the true state of the individual's heart:

They went out from us, but they were not of us; for if
they had been of us, they would have continued with us.
But they went out, that it might become plain that they
all are not of us.
1 John 2:19

Note, however, that the pattern we see in the Bible for responding to professions of faith does not address people who have previously made false professions, especially not those who have done so repeatedly. Indeed, the pattern in the book of Acts is of those hearing the gospel for the first time. What then should be the response to a prodigal who once professed faith, turned from their profession, and now declares he has truly come to Christ?

Before addressing this question, it is important to recognize our response to another's profession will not determine their eternal destiny. God is the one who saves (Ephesians 2:8). Where the Lord has accomplished a regenerating work in the heart of an individual and granted them the gift of saving faith, no act of man will ever pluck them out of the Father's hand (John 10:29). You need not fear that the eternal destiny of your prodigal rests in your right response to their profession.

While we should always encourage positive spiritual steps in the life of another, you cannot ignore a history of false professions. I am convinced that anyone who has truly come to repentance will see this himself. Think about it—what greater shame could one hold than having previously made a false profession to Jesus, the one to whom you now profess allegiance? You can approach with caution such a profession without outright rejection. There is much difference between saying, "You declared your faith in Jesus previously, what have you experienced differently this time?" versus, "You've said that before, why should I believe you this time?" Caution does not mean rejection.

REPENTANCE AND CONSEQUENCES

Perhaps the earliest test of a prodigal's newly professed faith will be whether he expects the immediate disappearance of all the consequences of his sinful choices. A truly broken soul who has come to repentance will not expect to be treated as though the past did not happen. The prayer of the prophet in Daniel 9 beautifully expresses the repentant heart's acceptance of the temporal consequences of sin. In looking upon the plight of his people, he acknowledged "the curse and oath that are written in the Law of Moses the servant of God have been poured out upon us, because we have sinned against him" (v. 11b). Moreover, forgiveness of past offenses does not immediately rebuild trust. Rebuilding trust takes time, and the individual needs to prove himself to be trustworthy.

The spouse of a prodigal seeking restoration faces especially difficult questions. Having walked with others on this road, my wife and I have seen the utter destruction a false profession brings to a family. In their excitement at the profession, it is easy for the spouse, friends, and others to ignore warning signs. Few things are as joyous as a marriage restored. Those navigating these difficult waters should seek wise, seasoned counsel. It is reasonable to expect one who has repeatedly betrayed trust to show their trustworthiness over time. True faith will weather the challenge of bearing the weight of progressive steps in restoration—and such a process will often expose a false profession.[17]

It is tempting, but unwise, for loved ones of prodigals to jump in and immediately try to fix everything for their offspring when he professes faith in Jesus. Even a person coming to faith in Christ has much to learn about the nature of sowing and reaping. The inclination to swoop in and make everything right in a prodigal's life by paying fines, covering legal fees, buying them a car, greasing the wheels for a job, and a myriad of other things is unlikely to be in the best long-term interests of the prodigal. Embrace the profession of faith, stand at his side as he seeks to put the pieces back together; but be cautious about fixing things yourself. Persevering in the trial of unscrambling the mess his life has become may be the very test to prove to you both the veracity of his profession of faith.

Dealing with Betrayal

Sometimes, the refusal to make everything right—often via an infusion of cash—will cause the prodigal to turn in anger and reveal his profession was merely a means to loosen the purse strings. He knows you well enough to know the desires of your heart, and your prodigal hopes by playing the faith card he will get what he wants. You will probably feel a deep sense of anger and frustration when his scheme is exposed. At such times, you need to take care of your own heart. Bitterness can seep in and consume you.

There are many warnings against bitterness in the Bible. We are instructed to "[l]et all bitterness ... be put away from you" (Ephesians 4:31). Furthermore, we are told of the importance of obtaining "the grace of God; that no root of bitterness springs up and causes trouble, and by it many become defiled" (Hebrews

---

17 Progressive restoration, in terms of their enjoyment of the full relationship of the family, does not violate the call in 2 Corinthians 2:5-8 and Galatians 6:1 to forgive and restore those who have fallen. Restoration into the fellowship of the church should be immediate. Restoration into the *full freedoms and responsibilities of familial and church relationships may need to be progressive.*

12:15). Bitterness is a cancer to the soul. It will wreak havoc on our spiritual life. We must guard against it.

How do we deal with the sense of betrayal that the false profession has aroused? By putting ourselves in our proper place. After all, who is really offended in such situations? Is not the sting of betrayal directed against our heavenly Father? Isn't he the one aggrieved? Moreover, have we not ourselves, in many of life's choices, repeatedly betrayed him as well? While not persistently or irrevocably, does this excuse even our momentary betrayals? The offense is actually against God. Therefore, we can leave it in his hands to address. We can push past the disappointment and the embarrassment of revealing to others that the joy we expressed to them has turned to sorrow again—but we must not allow bitterness to grow in our hearts.

A false profession is a painful reality not limited to our prodigal. It provokes sadness when it rears its ugly head. You are neither the first nor the last to experience its sting. Remember, Jesus knows the pain of such betrayal.

But Jesus said to him, "Judas, would you betray the Son of Man with a kiss?"
Luke 22:48

8

Battling Anger and Bitterness

It was a six-hour drive—unplanned and unwanted. Yet it was the right thing to do. A few hours into the journey, conviction gripped me as I realized there was within my heart a growing anger. Sinful anger. I had to miss several important activities at the university, requiring others on my leadership team to cover for me to free my schedule for this unexpected trip. As the highway road markers rolled by, my mind scrolled through the implications of this absence over the next few days. It was the beginning of an academic year—meaning I would miss several important events where I was scheduled to speak to new students in our undergraduate, professional, and graduate programs. Frustration flowed from the fact that it was so unnecessary. Anger soon swelled within me, dominating my thoughts and drawing my heart to a dark place.

We had received a phone call from a hospital in Iowa informing us of our son's admission to an intensive care unit. His drug use precipitated an acute lung problem. The prognosis was good, but he was very ill at present. Naturally, we dropped everything to go see him in the hospital and assess his need for aftercare. This was one of many emergency trips we made over the years when he was hospitalized to treat acute health problems associated with illicit drug use. We found it hard to avoid the grip of anger in response to the repeated trips, disrupted schedules, and added expenses—all due to his self-destructive behavior.

It is probably inevitable that parents of prodigals will struggle with anger over the endless impact of the destructive choices of their wayward son or daughter. Their manipulation, lies, and repeated efforts to use you to their advantage can provoke an anger you never thought a parent could have toward their child. If not checked, this anger will damage your other relationships, impair your ability to reach out in love to your prodigal, and jeopardize your spiritual health. To avoid its destructive consequences in our lives, we must understand the nature of anger, assess what has caused it to rise within us, and address it quickly when it is sinful.

ANGER UNDERSTOOD

Anger begins as an emotional response to a perceived injustice. It is neither premeditated nor necessarily sinful. On several occasions, our sinless Savior responded with anger (John 2:13-19; Mark 3:5). In like manner, many passages in the Old Testament speak of the anger of the Lord (Deuteronomy 9:20; 1 Kings 11:9). Indeed, Scripture warns: "Be angry and sin not; do not let the sun go down on your anger" (Ephesians 4:26).

Anger may lead to sin, but it is not always sinful. It is the expected response to injustice and unrighteousness. It can give stimulus to right action, such as when Jesus cleared the temple of merchants. This emotive response may move us to protect the innocent or vulnerable when they are oppressed by the powerful. It can cause us to flee from those things offensive to our holy God. Anger can serve as an alert system to provoke us to necessary action.

At the same time, Paul's warning in Ephesians 4:26 reminds us that anger can also provoke sin in our hearts. He zeroes in on the danger of allowing anger to fester in our hearts. Dwelling on things that precipitate anger can take our heart to unhealthy places. In particular, he tells us not to take our anger with us to bed, for in doing so we provide "opportunity to the devil" (v. 27). It is easy to understand why, as most of us have likely disobeyed this command from time to time and taken anger to bed with us. In the quiet and darkness of our bedchamber, we ruminate on how the offense provoking our anger has inconvenienced, embarrassed, or hurt us. What began as righteous indignation can descend into self-righteous thoughts and self-pity. The actions that self-righteousness and self-pity provoke are always sinful.

Do not miss the seriousness of Paul's statement in Ephesians 4:27. When anger festers, it is not only the flesh drawing us down a sinful path, it also provides an open door for the enemy of our soul. This warning should serve as a blaring siren in our ears about the depth of the danger ahead when we allow anger to fester.

Anger Assessed

While emotions like anger are spontaneous, they may also reveal inner flaws. Just as spilling an amber-colored bottle shows what is actually inside, the spillover of our emotions often uncovers the state of our heart. Getting angry without justification reveals wrong thinking and, perhaps, a deeper heart problem.

How do you assess whether anger is a sinful response or righteous indignation? It is rooted in the cause or focus of your anger. If it is a reaction to an injustice, such as the powerful preying upon the vulnerable, it expresses the heart of God. Often, however, our anger arises because we were inconvenienced, embarrassed, or otherwise put-upon by the actions of another. When our prodigal provokes anger within us, we must seek to understand why. Is it because their offense is an action against God, or because they have disrupted our plans and priorities?

Self-righteousness will be our common default mode in such circumstances. When gripped by anger, it is hard to discern the root cause of our response. We need to humbly ask the Lord to reveal the state of our heart. Only then can we probe the inner man with needed care. The root cause of our anger must be assessed with full honesty if it is to be effectively addressed.

Anger Addressed

When my heart was moved because an action by my son was an offense to God, my reaction was most often one of sadness more than anger. Most occasions of anger arose from embarrassment at the public nature of his escapades, the disruption to my own plans, or the unnecessary use of my resources. In other words, the occasion for anger came from my own selfishness. This made my anger sinful. Like all sin, it needed to be acknowledged as sinful, confessed, and repented from. I presume most loved ones of prodigals struggle in the same vein as I. Herein lies a danger. Sinful actions by our prodigal can provoke sin in our own hearts. Their folly places our heart at risk, as our flesh may drive our response. This can also provide an open door for the devil to send us into a dark place. We must recognize this reality and be on our guard. In fact, the deeper the destructive hole our prodigal digs, the greater the danger is that we fall into a pit of anger. While the sins of a prodigal may draw us into many different sinful responses, anger is perhaps the most common.

A prodigal is accountable for the sinful choice provoking our anger, but *we* are accountable for our response to their choice. Their sinful action does not justify a sinful response on our behalf. We must never excuse our sin because it was provoked by the sin of another. When confronted with our sinful response—either internally, by the Spirit's conviction, or by someone else—we must stop when the words "Yes, but" arise in our heads or flow from our lips. We must not allow ourselves to seek justification for a sinful response—in reality, there is none.

How does one turn from sinful anger when it burns at the edges of our heart? We must turn wrong thinking to righteous thinking if we are to bring about the change needed in our hearts. We must make "every thought captive to obey Christ" (2 Corinthians 10:5). The Word of God must be the lens through which we evaluate our thinking. We cannot trust our own hearts. There is too much corruption remaining within us. The apostle Paul declared, "I do not understand my own actions. For I do not do what I want, but I do the very thing I hate" (Romans 7:15).

We must use the Word of God to assess the reason for our response, including the wrong thinking behind it. It may be true that the need arising from their destructive choices has inconvenienced us and disrupted our plans, but is this the big deal we make it to be? How do we know if our plans would have come to fruition? Scripture warns us,

> *Come now, you who say, "Today or tomorrow we will*
> *go into such and such town and spend a year there and*

*trade and make a profit"—yet you do not know what
tomorrow will bring. What is your life? For you are a
mist that appears for a little time and then vanishes.
Instead you ought to say, "If the Lord wills, we will live
and do this or that."*
James 4:13-15

What we see as a disruption of our plans may be used by God to accomplish a greater purpose. Joseph did not plan to become a slave, a captive to Potiphar in the land of Egypt. Over time he could see the divine purpose of his captivity and later declare to his brothers, "As for you, you meant evil against me, but God meant it for good, to bring it about that many people should be kept alive, as they are today" (Genesis 50:20).

Furthermore, though the public nature of our prodigal's actions may have brought embarrassment to our family, should it matter what others think? Did not Paul declare, "But with me it is a very small thing that I should be judged by you or by any human court" (1 Corinthians 4:3)? When we respond with anger due to public embarrassment, is this not the response of a prideful heart? We may feel ashamed because we think others are judging us for not parenting our prodigal well. Are we not giving over to the fear of man? Does the Word of God show us a better way?

DEALING WITH BITTERNESS

Some Christians who have walked a long journey with a prodigal have allowed anger to dominate their lives. In their deep disappointment and embarrassment at the reckless choices of their prodigal, they have turned their focus to their personal injuries. Some loved ones of prodigals fall into the trap of creating a mental catalogue of the offenses they have had to bear. They rehearse the wrongs and often share them with others. Soon, bitterness becomes the dominant attitude toward their prodigal, readily spilling over to the rest of life. If you find yourself in a place where anger has morphed into a root of bitterness, take radical action to dig it out of the depths of your heart.

You must see it for the sin it is and make full confession. Humbly and openly, come before God. Though better known for his preaching and teaching ministry, his giftedness as a songwriter comes through in the powerful lyrics written by Don Carson in his song, "I Am Ashamed," which can help take you on the path to healing:

> *I used to nurture bitterness,*
> *To count up every slight.*
> *The world's a moral wilderness,*
> *And I have felt its blight.*
> *Self pity ruled, resentment reigned;*
> *No one understood my pain.*
> *I spiraled down in murky night,*
> *Insisting that I had the right*
> *To hate and hate again.*
>
> *But then the gospel taught me how*
> *To contemplate the cross.*
> *For there Christ died for me—and now*
> *I've glimpsed the bitter cost.*
> *He bore abuse, and blows, and hate;*
> *He did not retaliate.*
> *Triumphant malice sneered and tossed*
> *Blind rage at him—he never lost*
> *The love that conquers hate.*
>
> *To make no threat, to smile, forgive,*
> *To love—and not because I must.*
> *For Jesus showed me how to live*
> *And trust the One who's just;*
> *To suffer wrong and feel the pain,*
> *Certain that the loss is gain—*
> *O God I want so much to trust,*
> *To follow Jesus on the cross,*
> *To love and love again.*

I am ashamed;
O, my Lord, forgive.[18]

We must be forceful in dealing with sinful anger in our hearts, because anger is a powerful emotion. It can lead us down a road we should not travel. Jesus gave us pointed warnings of the dangers of anger:

> *You have heard that it was said to those of old, "You shall not murder; and whoever murders will be liable to judgment." But I say to you that everyone who is angry with his brother will be liable to judgment.*
> **Matthew 5:21-22**

Festering anger is serious business. Do not let it find a home in your heart. Battle against it when you are provoked by the choices of your prodigal. Instead, we should pray, "Lord, use this to show the love of Christ to my prodigal. May my actions bear witness for You before all who watch my response." Rest assured, others are watching.

> *See that no one repays anyone evil for evil, but always seek to do good to one another and everyone.*
> **1 Thessalonians 5:15**

---

18 "I Am Ashamed," Lyrics by D. A. Carson, © Drink Your Tea Music, 2016.

9

KINDLING AFFECTION FOR YOUR PRODIGAL

"I love you Dad." The words spilled readily from my son's lips, but a reply did not quickly flow from mine. His call was yet another attempt to manipulate us to get money he undoubtedly would use for drugs. My hesitancy was not because I questioned my love for him. Rather, it arose because at this moment I did not feel much affection for him. The constant lies. The continual efforts to manipulate us. The efforts to make us feel guilty so we would do as he asked. The threats of bad things that were sure to happen to him if we did not fork over the cash. These made our hearts weary of his calls. His glib expression of love seemed hypocritical.

Those with offspring immersed in a destructive lifestyle will inevitably struggle with periods where they lose affection for their son or daughter. Siblings, spouses, and children of prodigals may experience the same loss of affection. We dislike—and are even repulsed by—what he has become. Sometimes it seems as if another has possessed both body and soul of our loved one. The ugliness of his life and behavior dulls warm feelings that were once so strong. This reality can itself produce feelings of guilt. It is hard to be affectionate toward one who has embraced a lifestyle offensive to the One you love most.

Parents who have never known life with a prodigal will likely recoil at the words written above. They may wonder how any parent can lose affection for their offspring. Believe me, it happens. If you have not known the depths of degradation of life with a prodigal, it is understandable you would view a loss of affection to be unthinkable. However, when your child has become a stranger, the link to the adorable past is hard to sustain. It takes a conscious effort to love, instead of becoming apathetic or bitter towards them.

In the days of deepest agony after our son's death, I found myself repeatedly asking God to restore our memories of his younger years. In particular, the joy he brought to us during that period of his life. When we held a small gathering in our home instead of a regular funeral, my prayer request to those gathered was that God would grant this desire. Years of betrayal and rejection readily leave such memories in the dust. Nevertheless, it is right that we work to regain or sustain the memories and the affection. For, rebellious or not, they are our children.

Jesus displayed an affection for the wayward. Consider his lament over Jerusalem:

> *O Jerusalem, Jerusalem, the city that kills the prophets*
> *and stones those who are sent to it! How often would I*
> *have gathered your children together as a hen gathers*
> *her brood under her wings, and you were not willing!*
> **Matthew 23:37**

A geographical place does not kill or stone to kill. It does not have children. Jesus was not referring to the physical city but to its inhabitants. His reference was to its inhabitants over generations. Rebellious and wayward as they were, he felt a deep affection for these people. His heartache for them leaps off the page as you read these words. He presents his longing to care for them in a most tender way—as a hen covers her brood with her wings.

Consider his response to the rich young ruler:

> *And as he was setting out on his journey, a man ran up*
> *and knelt before him and asked him, "Good Teacher,*
> *what must I do to inherit eternal life?" And Jesus said to*
> *him, "Why do you call me good? No one is good except*
> *God alone. You know the commandments: 'Do not*
> *murder, Do not commit adultery, Do not steal, Do not*
> *bear false witness, Do not defraud, Honor your father*
> *and mother.'" And he said to him, "Teacher, all these I*
> *have kept from my youth." And Jesus, looking at him,*

loved him, and said to him, "You lack one thing: go, sell all that you have and give to the poor, and you will have treasure in heaven; and come, follow me." Disheartened by the saying, he went away sorrowful, for he had great possessions.

Mark 10:17-22

Doesn't Jesus' affection for this wayward young ruler exude from the passage as you read it? Do you not sense his care—and, in turn, his sadness at the rejection? In the parallel passage in Luke, the beloved physician tells us Jesus looked at him "with sadness" (Luke 18:24). He did not compromise the truth to accommodate the young man's desired lifestyle. Rather, Jesus confronted him with the greatest barrier in his life—his riches. Despite the man's misplaced love for money, Jesus held an obvious affection for this young ruler.

It is true that there are some for whom Jesus displayed no positive affection. In particular, false teachers. His words boldly condemned the scribes and Pharisees: "But woe to you scribes and Pharisees, hypocrites!" (Matthew 23:13). Seven times he declares ruin upon them with such words. He expressed no warm feelings for this group who led others astray and oppressed them with their man-made rules. Yet even his frank statement of woe upon them may be heard as an act of love, serving as a stunning warning of their perilous state if they do not repent. With most sinners, Jesus exhibited a tenderness even in his rebukes (for example, the Samaritan woman at the well in John 4).

Affection, in the sense of tenderness or filial attachment, is a good thing. The apostle Paul commends us to show such tenderness toward one another in the body of Christ: "Love one another with brotherly affection" (Romans 12:10). Paul yearned for the saints in Philippi "with the affection of Christ Jesus" (Philippians 1:8). Many have said that true love is not an emotion—rather, it is an act of giving something of yourself for another. Jesus said, "Greater love has no one than this, that someone lays down his life for his friends" (John 15:13). While this is true, the Bible also commends showing affection with this love. Affection is a positive emotional bond for another producing a heartfelt compassion for them. As this is good and right to feel toward those in God's forever family, it is also good and right in biological families.

How does one sustain or recapture affection when your prodigal is driving your affection to the deepest recesses of your being?

REFRAIN FROM REHEARSING THEIR SINFUL ACTIONS

Nothing will dull your affections for something or someone more quickly than focusing on their unattractive elements. Be cautious about lamenting to one another the latest foibles of your prodigal or recalling those of the past. Reviewing the sinful ways of your prodigal will drive a wedge between your heart and the affection you should have. 1 Peter 4:8 reminds us that "love covers a multitude of sins." In his helpful commentary, John MacArthur states, "it seems best to understand the phrase here as a general axiom."[19] God's love covers sin through the offering of his son. Christians cover sin by forgiving and forgetting, which would exclude rehearsing.

Some may ask, "Can I truly forget the sinful episodes and pain of our prodigal's life?" The science on our ability to forget, as in erase completely from our memory, is both complex and unsettled. Regardless, the Bible indicates we can forget painful episodes in our lives. Joseph even named his son over the blessing of forgetfulness:

> *Joseph called the name of the first-born Manasseh. "For,"*
> *he said, "God has made me forget all my hardship and all*
> *my father's house."*
> **Genesis 41:51**

Was Joseph declaring his experiences as a captive—both slave and prisoner—was wiped from his memory bank? Probably not. But they did not dwell in the forefront of his mind. They had no front seat in his panoramic view of life. Therefore, they did not serve as a continuing source of anguish nor color his view of his

---

19   John F. MacArthur. *The MacArthur New Testament Commentary—1 Peter*. (Chicago, Ill. Moody Publishers, 2004), 241.

brothers when they later appeared in Egypt. Instead, the blessings of God occupied the front seat of his mind. These served as the lens through which he viewed his life experience.

Moreover, there are many instances in the Bible where the Lord warned people not to forget something—giving plain indication that forgetting is possible. Consider his words in Deuteronomy 4:9:

> *Only take care, and keep your soul diligently, lest you forget the things that your eyes have seen, and lest they depart from your heart all the days of your life. Make them known to your children and your children's children.*

The issue is not forgetting in the sense of reaching a point of being unable to recall them. Rather, it is to keep these things in the forefront of your mind. Make certain they color how you see the world in which you live, and guide your steps. This is how they will serve as a lamp unto your feet (Psalm 119:105).

To argue that we cannot truly forget something is to place a meaning on the word beyond its biblical meaning. The admonition to forget is not a call to extinguish the existence of the events from your mind so as to never recall them again. Instead, it is a call to no longer dwell on the matter or give it a place of prominence in your thoughts. It is also a call not to use the painful events in your child's life as a filter through which you judge the circumstances of your life. Wouldn't rehearsing your prodigal's painful episodes contradict this call?

The "telling" of your prodigal's latest misadventures to others should also be as limited as possible. Proverbs 17:9 reminds us "whoever covers an offense seeks love, but he who repeats a matter separates close friends." When others ask how our child is doing, it is not helpful to anyone to share the most recent horror story. I suppose we may find some measure of relief to get it off our chest and engender the empathy of the listener. Far more helpful is to focus on the reality that your prodigal remains far from God, so you would appreciate their continued prayers for wisdom for you and God's mercy for your prodigal. There are times when details should be shared with others, but give careful thought before doing so. It is unhealthy for you to rehearse those tragic choices.

EMBRACE THINGS THAT ENHANCE YOUR AFFECTION

The Old Testament provides extensive ceremonial instructions for Israel. These ceremonies were designed to keep fresh the memories of the things God did in the past. We are forgetful beings, with perhaps the exception of those times when we have been offended. Memories gather dust over time and become more difficult to access. Rehearsing important things keeps those memories fresh. When those memories are of blessed times with individuals, our affections for them are strengthened. Paul told the Philippians to think on things that are true, honorable, just, pure, lovely, commendable, and praiseworthy (Philippians 4:8). Should it surprise us that this admonition comes after pointed instruction is given to two people in conflict with each other?

How you think about your prodigal, in terms of the things upon which you meditate and verbally rehearse, will influence your affection for him. Do what you must to kindle affection through right thinking and actions. Since affection is an expression of our emotional selves, the specifics will vary with the individual.

I found reviewing old photos of our son's younger years to be heartwarming and a reminder of my deep affection for him. Those same photos brought sadness for my wife. It was not good for her to review them, as they brought deeper pain. For her, giving place for her motherly instincts provided a means to sustain affection in some of the darkest times of his life. Whether that meant preparing or buying a special food or beverage, or purchasing needed apparel, these actions helped her hold affection. Doing something special for him that a mother would naturally do was helpful in sustaining her affection. We needed to give each other the freedom to find those things that would stoke the fire of affection for him within us.

Each loved one will need to find the means of kindling affection for a prodigal that works for them. You may need to be creative. But if you don't, affection will probably wither away before you realize it.

ACKNOWLEDGE THAT HE IS MADE IN THE IMAGE OF GOD

Of the many things often lost in modern debates about the early chapters of Genesis, few are as unfortunate as our loss of the reality that all humans were made in the image of God. The image-bearing nature of every human being is the foundation of the sanctity of human life. We should view all people through this truth. Though the defiling dust of the road on which they travel may dull its sheen, your prodigal is an image bearer of our Creator. It is proper to long for the removal of the dust and pray that God would allow the image in which they were made to shine forth.

People are quick to make value judgments about others based on their actions. We tend to dismiss as unworthy of our time or energy those who offend us by their words or deeds. This is a sad mistake. There are times when we need to let others go, even a loved one who is a prodigal. Letting them go means ceasing our effort to restrain their choices and the consequences those choices bring. Their choices may require creating a measure of distance between our lives and theirs for a time. But we should not forsake them—in the sense of forever washing our hands of them and bidding them good riddance. We have known of parents, siblings, and children of prodigals who have taken such a stand. They have allowed the pain caused by their prodigal to cause them to forget the image-bearing nature of this one who has wounded them so deeply. If you have taken this stance with a prodigal, you must recognize this is a sinful response. It suggests bitterness has taken root in your heart. We must never dismiss the life of another human being. For the Christian, declaring, "I don't care what happens to them" is not an option.

Ultimately, our affection is rooted in the essence of their being. The affection Jesus showed the rich young ruler who walked away was grounded in the image-bearing nature of the rich young man. His corrupted flesh hid the sheen of this glorious truth. But our Savior saw beyond the corrupted layer on the surface. We must do the same with our prodigals. Remember, their image-bearing nature is rooted in their creation, not their conduct.

ACCEPT HIM AS UNIQUELY CRAFTED BY GOD

Along with the loss of commitment to the sanctity of life, modern society also rejects the intimate involvement of our Creator in the molding of each newborn child. As biomedical science has increased our understanding of the processes of conception and the development of the unborn child, the active role of the Creator in each child has—in the minds of many—been pushed aside as a quaint and outdated notion. Our confidence in our medical techniques to manipulate conception has led to the belief that we control the when, where, and to whom a child enters this world. While not consciously embracing this view, it is easy for Christians to lose their sense of understanding that each individual was fearfully and wonderfully made. Yet Scripture could not be clearer:

> You formed my inward parts; you knitted me together
> in my mother's womb. I praise you, for I am fearfully
> and wonderfully made. Wonderful are your works; my
> soul knows it very well. My frame was not hidden from
> you when I was being made in secret, intricately woven
> in the depths of the earth. Your eyes saw my unformed
> substance; in your book were written, every one of them,
> the days that were formed for me, when as yet there was
> none of them.
> **Psalm 139:13-16**

Your loved one who has strayed so far is not a product of random processes. An unseen hand of fate will not determine his days. The Lord we serve and love knit him together in the womb and determined his days before we ever held him in our arms. His chosen path has taken him far from God, but he is God's unique creation nonetheless. Never forget the Creator made him and put him in your life. He has done so purposefully. The intertwining of your lives, though perhaps painful at present, is a part of God's sovereign plan for both you and your child. Let this truth sink into your hearts, for you to remember in the most difficult days.

Adoptive parents of children who have chosen the path of a prodigal especially need to learn to rest on God's sovereignty. Adoption is a marvelous picture of the grace shown to us when we were adopted into God's forever family. Yet we have known adoptive parents of prodigals who concluded their choice to adopt must have been wrong because of their child's rebellion. Some have, in turn, washed their hands of these adopted children. It is critical to understand that the path chosen by an adopted child neither validates nor invalidates the original choice to adopt him or her. An adopted child enters a home under the same control of the sovereign King of the universe as does any biological offspring. Their entrance into your home and into your lives was not a mistake. You must not treat your relationship with them as though it was.

Ask God to Work in Your Heart

Because our prodigal has surrendered to the flesh, we must recognize our flesh will incline us to respond to him sinfully. Are we not prone to return in kind the wounds inflicted by others? This is why we should mimic the cry of David: "Search me, O God, and know my heart! Try me and know my thoughts! And see if there be any grievous way in me, and lead me in the way everlasting!" (Psalm 139:23-24). A willingness to check our feelings toward our prodigal on a regular basis will go a long way in making sure our heart is where it should be in regard to him. It is an essential step in kindling affection for him.

"And may the Lord make you increase and abound in love for one another and for all."
1 Thessalonians 3:12

10

BEING CONTENT WITH THE SOVEREIGN CHOICES OF GOD

It was a joyous holiday gathering, with family members delighting in the company of one another. Holiday decorations, music, and food abounded; parents with a wonderful marriage rooted in their faith in Christ; children who love the Lord, and whose spouses love and serve him as well; grandchildren raised in the nurture and admonition of the Lord. The scene was just what we expected our family to be. Only, it wasn't our family. My wife and I were guests in their holiday celebration, thoughtfully and lovingly included as "adopted" members of the family. As I bathed in the warmth of the gathering, I felt a painful twinge in my heart. God had not blessed our family with a similar godly heritage—offspring who were all walking with the Lord. How do I live with this painful reality? How do I forestall feelings of envy or jealousy that regretfully sometimes arise in such moments?

Just as the shepherd searched only for the lost one of the hundred sheep, the mind of a parent often draws with laser focus on the *lost* child in the family. The burden of his state is a great weight to bear. The pain draws you to prayer with great persistence and intensity. It is easy to focus on what you do not have and miss the full enjoyment of the blessings you do have. Our flesh tempts us to envy those who have been spared such struggles.

How do you battle not only wistful feelings, but also feelings of envy and jealousy that raise their ugly heads from within? You should keep a watchful eye to identify them when they appear and redirect your mind to think about godly things. This strategy may need to be deployed on various occasions. This will require learning contentment with the sovereign choices of God. Even the hard choices.

CREATOR, SUSTAINER, AND RULER

Developing contentment in the sovereign choices of God requires us to start at the beginning. The literal beginning. It is unfortunate that so much focus on Genesis 1 in our generation has been on debating the how and when of God's creative act in bringing this earth into being. Those are important questions. Unfortunately, such a focus may cause us to miss the forest for the trees. The fundamental issue in Genesis 1 is not how or when—but who.

Those unfamiliar with the history of science and philosophy may not recognize the profundity of this simple declaration in Genesis 1:1— "In the beginning, God created the heavens and the earth." Ancient philosophers, such as Aristotle, and millennia of scientists, all embraced what is sometimes called the steady state theory of the universe. Simply put, what exists has existed forever. There was no beginning. It always was as it is. When, in 1927, astronomer Georges Lemaitre put forth his notion that the universe had a singular beginning, it represented a refutation of a perspective held by many for thousands of years. Further astronomical research has provided compelling evidence for a singular beginning of the universe, referred to by many as the Big Bang Theory. Few today oppose the notion of a point in time in which the universe unfolded in all its unfathomable vastness.

Though it took thousands of years for philosophers and scientists to concur, the book of Genesis declares the universe has not always existed. Scripture unapologetically proclaims it came into being at a point in time by the creative act of God. All that was, is, and ever shall be, flows from his creative power. Subsequent verses in Genesis declare his intimate engagement in shaping the earth for the crown of his creation—humanity.

Scripture shows that our God remains engaged in his creation. He did not, like one who spins a top and then steps back to watch its course, just create it and walk away. The Lord continues his intimate involvement in this marvelous creation as a gardener who waters and prunes. Speaking of the Second person of the Trinity, the Lord Jesus, the book of Hebrews declares, "he upholds the universe by the word of his power" (Hebrews 1:3).

The picture painted in Scripture is of a physical world that would collapse apart from his continued power to uphold it. Not only is God the Creator, he is also the Sustainer. His sustaining work is not limited to the incalculable power needed to uphold the inestimable vastness of the universe. This power is also deployed to meet the needs of all life on this speck of dust on which we dwell:

> *Look at the birds of the air: they neither sow nor reap*
> *nor gather into barns, and yet your heavenly Father*
> *feeds them*
> *... But if God so clothes the grass of the field, which today*
> *is alive and tomorrow is thrown into the oven, will he not*
> *much more clothe you, O you of little faith?*
> **Matthew 6:26, 30**

The God who made it all controls it all. Yet he does not simply control, he tends to its needs. He cares for those who dwell on the earth. It is part of his work as ruler over all.

Even physical earthly events often ascribed to chance are under his control. We sometimes speak of chance as though it were an ethereal force controlling physical phenomenon. Chance is simply the probability of an event occurring in the natural order of things, apart from God supernaturally intervening and changing that natural order momentarily. Hence, meteorologists will tell us what is the chance of rain tomorrow. But neither the meteorologist nor chance will *determine* whether it rains. The Bible tells us God "sends rain on the just and on the unjust" (Matthew 5:45). Astronomers may tell us precisely what time dawn will arrive one month from today. Nonetheless, it is God who "makes his sun rise on the evil and on the good" (Matthew 5:45). Gravity, friction, wind resistance, and the force of the throw may seem to determine the chance of the roll of a die coming up six, but Proverbs tells us that "the lot is cast into the lap, but its every decision is from the LORD" (16:33). The apostles understood the intimate role of the sovereignty of God in all events on this earth. This is why, when choosing between two men equally qualified to replace Judas, they selected by lots—for they knew God was in control of the outcome (Acts 1:21-26). Oh, that we would have the understanding of and confidence in the sovereignty of God displayed by the apostles! Nothing happens by chance. There is neither the luck of the draw nor accidents of nature. It is all under his control.

His control even extends to the kingdoms of the world. Through the prophet Daniel, the Lord God declares that "the Most High rules the kingdom of men and gives it to whom he will and sets over it the lowliest of men" (Daniel 4:17). Civil society is also under God's sovereign control. The reality is "there is no authority except from God, and those that exist have been instituted by God" (Romans 13:1). Democratic elections and military coups notwithstanding, the Lord ultimately controls who rules in the realm of human society.

Consider the account of Mary and Joseph. As they awaited the birth of the one foretold by angelic announcement, they dwelt in Nazareth—about twenty miles from the place of prophetic fulfillment. The prophet Micah foretold hundreds of years earlier that the Messiah would be born in Bethlehem (Micah 5:2). The Lord could have sent Gabriel again, telling them to go to Bethlehem. Instead, the *one* who is sovereign over all moved in the heart of Caesar Augustus to order a census of the whole world. In so doing, Mary and Joseph were compelled to relocate to the very town the prophet declared as the birthplace of the Messiah. They arrived at just the right time for her to give birth while there. Are we not foolish when we forget or doubt the intimate control of our heavenly Father in the affairs of human society? The Bible repeatedly shows that our God orchestrates every stanza in the score of human history.

No one can understand how the choices of men and the sovereignty of God intersect. Why would one think that the actions of God are understandable? If you could fully understand God, the how and why behind his actions—what would that make you? Equal to God? Surely, we should expect elements of mystery when it comes to the ways of God. Like Job, we must acknowledge there are things about the work of God "too wonderful for me" (Job 42:3b). While it is beyond our complete understanding, the plain truth of the Bible—declared from beginning to end—is that God is sovereign in all the affairs of men. Physical, civil, and spiritual affairs.

Sovereign in Salvation

We have already considered, in chapter 2, biblical truths showing God's sovereignty in the spiritual fruit born in this world. In his marvelous discussion of the sovereign choice of God in the salvation of the Jews in Romans 9 through 11, Paul reminds his readers that in the days of Elijah the prophet, the Lord had kept for himself a remnant of faithful people in Israel (11:2-4). He then declares: "So too at the present time there is a remnant, chosen by grace" (Romans 11:5). There was a remnant of Israel who were faithful to the calling of God, of which Paul was a part. They were the fruit of God's sovereign choice. A manifestation of his grace. And so it is with all who are saved:

For many are called, but few are chosen.
Matthew 22:14

No one can come to me unless the Father who sent me draws him.
John 6:44

He chose us in him before the foundation of the world....
In love he predestined us for adoption through Jesus Christ, according to the purpose of his will.
Ephesians 1:4-5

For we know, brothers loved by God, that he has chosen you.
1 Thessalonians 1:4

> *But you are a chosen race, a royal priesthood, a holy*
> *nation, a people for his own possession.*
> **1 Peter 2:9**

Others have with greater care and skill unfolded Scriptures demonstrating the sovereign choice of God in salvation.[20] None has stated this truth more concisely than J.I. Packer, who reminds us that God "shows His freedom and lordship by discriminating between sinners, causing some to hear the gospel, while others do not hear it, and moving some of those who hear it to repentance while leaving others in their unbelief; thus teaching His saints that He owes mercy to none, and that it is entirely of His grace, not at all through their own effort, that they themselves have found life."[21]

Those who fail to embrace this biblical truth will likely struggle with finding contentment when the new birth they hoped to see in their child does not come to fruition. Contentment does not mean you cease to plead for the soul of your wayward child, spouse, sibling, or parent. It does not mean you stop your active pursuit of his spiritual well-being. Paul passionately yearned for the salvation of his fellow Israelites. Indeed, he said he had "great sorrow and unceasing anguish" in his heart for the Jews (Romans 9:2). Furthermore, he said that he wished he "were accursed and cut off from Christ for the sake of my brothers, my kinsmen according to the flesh" (Romans 9:3).

Paul did not give up hope nor desist from longing for his fellow Israelites to come into God's forever family. But who would deny that the portrait of Paul provided in Scripture is one of a man who displayed profound contentment with the sovereign choices of God in his life? While he longed for the salvation of his kinsmen, as shown in Romans 9 through 11, he did not blame God for their failure to come to Christ nor express jealously at the responsiveness of the Gentiles. His own people rejected him when he presented the gospel in synagogues in city after city. In contrast, the Gentiles heard him with gladness. Despite disappointment in the failure of his kinsmen to respond, he rejoiced

20   For example, see J.I. Packer, *Evangelism & the Sovereignty of God,* (Downers Grove, Ill.: IVP, 1961), and R.C Sproul, *Chosen By God,* (Nashville, Tn.: 1986).

21   J.I. Packer, *Knowing God,* (Downers Grove, Ill.: 1973), 70-71.

in the fruit God brought forth. As the parent of a prodigal you will likely ask why God has not chosen your offspring for the blessing of salvation. You may even find yourself on the slippery slope of questioning the rightness of God for his failure to call your loved one. The apostle Paul had some pointed words for those who raise such questions,

> But who are you, O man, to answer back to God? Will what is molded say to its molder, "Why have you made me like this?" Has the potter no right over the clay, to make of the same lump one vessel for honored use and another for dishonorable use? What if God, desiring to show his wrath and to make known his power, has endured with much patience vessels of wrath prepared for destruction, in order to make known the riches of his glory for vessels of mercy, which he has prepared beforehand for glory.
> **Romans 9:20-23**

Paul understood salvation was all in God's hands. He was in no position to judge the rightness of God's choices. While he yearned for those of the household of Israel who did not know Christ to believe, he rejoiced in the blessings of the Gentiles who had come to saving faith. Likewise, we should yearn and pray for the return of our prodigals as long as they and we have breath. Yet we should also be able to rejoice with those in whom God is working. It is not wrong to long to hear that your children are walking in the truth (3 John 4), but it is wrong to be jealous at hearing of the faithfulness of the children of others.

The fundamental question you must face is simple: Do you believe God is in control of all? Scripture declares the truth of his sovereignty from Genesis to Revelation. He controls all. He displays his control in his creation. He displays it in the rising and falling of the kingdoms of men. He also displays his sovereignty in those whom he calls for salvation. Jesus said to his disciples, "you did not choose me, but I chose you" (John 15:16). Elsewhere he proclaims, "All that the Father gives me will come to me" (John 6:37).

SOVEREIGNTY, TRUST, AND CONTENTMENT

I do not believe you can find true contentment in this life without unequivocally embracing the sovereignty of God in all things, including the salvation of souls. Contentment finds its foundation when we trust him with those choices. This is difficult. Instead of just sighing in deep resignation that God will do what he will do, you must learn to trust that what he is doing is good. His goodness is such that his sovereignty will be consistent with his holy purposes.

Job is a marvelous example of one who learned this experientially. The Sabeans killed his servants and stole his oxen and donkeys (Job 1:14-15). Fire from heaven burned up his sheep and the shepherds watching them (v. 16). The Chaldeans took his camels and murdered those watching them (v. 17). Finally, a great wind from the wilderness destroyed the house where his children were having a party—killing them all (v. 18). In staccato fashion, all but his wife and four servants died. He knew that both the enemies and the natural means were simply instruments of God, who was the *one* that eliminated almost all he possessed. "The LORD gave, and the LORD has taken away; blessed be the name of the LORD" (v. 21). Amazingly, "In all this Job did not sin or charge God with wrong" (v. 22).

This does not mean he did not struggle with these hard events. He struggled to the depth of his heart and mourned with a severity unknown in modern times. His soul was troubled to such a depth of despair that three friends came and joined him in a seven-day silent vigil, agonizing with him in his dreadful plight (2:11-13). Then, they made the mistake of opening their mouths. Accusations flew at Job from his friends' lips like fiery arrows of an invading force. Beaten down by his accusers, Job demands an audience with God, insisting the Sovereign One explain his actions. Then God visits Job in his pitiful state and places the wonder of his creative power before him. Job's eyes and understanding are opened. Thus, he declares,

I know that you can do all things, and that no purpose of yours can be thwarted.... I have uttered what I did not understand, things too wonderful for me.
Job 42:2, 3

Once again, Job came to a place of peace. There he not only knew, but also trusted, this Sovereign One who is in control of all things. Others in the Bible have found this peaceful place of trusting as well.

Mary's response to Elizabeth, the mother of John the Baptist, is one of the more marvelous expressions of praise in the Bible. It also is a wonderful expression of confident trust in the sovereignty of God's choices. The appearance of the angel Gabriel had troubled her soul greatly (Luke 1:29). His words that she was to conceive while betrothed must have troubled her further. The betrothal period was a bond as firm as marriage itself. To break it required a formal divorce.[22] To be found pregnant during this period that tested the fidelity of the betrothed would have, at best, left her a social outcast—at worse, the victim of a judicial stoning for adultery. From a human perspective, conceiving and bearing a child while betrothed would bring nothing but hardship. Indeed, Scripture implies that she and Jesus lived with persistent whispers of her presumed infidelity (cf. Matthew 13:55, John 8:41). Despite this foreboding future, she expressed the wondrous praise recorded by Luke and known as The Magnificat. Read and feel the pulse of her trust in God flowing through her words:

> *My soul magnifies the Lord, and my spirit rejoices in God my Savior, for he has looked on the humble estate of his servant. For behold, from now on all generations will call me blessed; for he who is mighty has done great things for me, and holy is his name. And his mercy is for those who fear him from generation to generation. He has shown strength in his arm; he has scattered the proud in the thoughts of their hearts; he has brought down the mighty from their thrones and exalted those of humble estate; he has filled the hungry with good things, and the rich he has sent empty away. He has helped his servant Israel, in remembrance of his mercy, as he spoke to our fathers, to Abraham and to his offspring forever.*
> **Luke 1:46-55**

---

22 John MacArthur, *The MacArthur New Testament Commentary*, Matthew 1-7 (Chicago, Ill.: Moody Press, 1985), 16-18.

Like Job and Mary, you can do more than accept the truth that God is sovereign—you can trust the choices he makes in his rule over all. He has shown many times how his goodness shines even in hard times. It is in this place of trust that you will find the true treasure of contentment—with not only your life and its losses, but also with the blessings he gives to others.

True contentment includes being able to rejoice in the blessings others have received, but which have been withheld from you. True contentment is the childless couple who is able to rejoice at the birth of the children of their friends. True contentment is the teenager in a wheelchair who is able to cheer for the accomplishments of his sister on the athletic field. And true contentment is the parent of a prodigal being able to rejoice in the faithful walk of their friends' children—or the spouse of a prodigal rejoicing in the restoration of the marriage of another. The angels rejoice over the salvation of sinners. We rightly join them in that rejoicing. Our friends properly rejoice in the goodness of God to their families. We do well to join them in giving him thanks. The blessing of God merits our praise regardless of where or upon whom it is bestowed.

> *Though the fig tree should not blossom, nor fruit be on the vines, the produce of the olive fail and the fields yield no food, the flock be cut off from the fold and there be no herd in the stalls, yet I will rejoice in the LORD, I will take joy in the God of my salvation.*
> **Habakkuk 3:17-18**

11

LIVING WITH THE SILENCE OF HEAVEN

The faint sound of weeping shook me out of the story in which I was engrossed. As I focused on the sound, I could discern a muffled, but intense weeping. I closed the book I was reading and walked down the hall to our study. Behind the closed door arose the clear sound of deep sadness. I opened the door and enveloped my crying wife into my arms. As her weeping subsided, she told me she was listening to a program when she heard a hymn declaring gratefulness for the mercy of God. A deep, rich truth. One that should cause every believer to deliver thanks to the God of heaven. But with the wound of our son's death so raw, it provoked in her inexpressible sadness and an understandable question. Despite our desperate prayers, why had God not shown our son mercy? For many years, it was our persistent cry—"Lord, be merciful to our son and save him from the destructive path he has chosen." However, God did not grant our earnest petition.

Any faithful parent or loved one of a prodigal has spent untold hours in agonizing prayer over the soul of their wayward child, spouse, sibling, or parent. With passion and persistence, they bring a plea for their prodigal's salvation before the throne of God. They recognize nothing else really matters. So, what happens to your prayer life when it becomes clear your plea for them was not answered in the way you hoped? How do you maintain confidence in the power of prayer when it appears to be missing when you needed and wanted it most? How does one deal with the silence of heaven? Times of prayer were arduous in the weeks following our son's death. I prayed for our children at least three times a day since each of their births. As I began every day in prayer after his death, I faced the painful reality there was one for whom I could no longer intercede in prayer. Each prayer time was a stark reminder—my most earnest prayer was, as far as we knew, answered with a "No." It is true we were not with our son in his final hours, so I cannot say with certainty he was not like the thief on the cross and experienced the grace of God in those hours. However, his persistent rejection of God's truth leaves us with no basis to hope for a deathbed conversion. We would be beyond delighted to experience surprise in heaven. Nevertheless, it is apparent to us that our earnest prayer went unanswered. Even if answered for his eternal benefit, our earthly experience remains one of a prodigal who never returned—of prayers unanswered.

We must focus on essential truths about prayer to recapture our confidence in prayer when we experience the silence of God. These truths are important whether your unanswered prayer is for the return of a prodigal, for physical healing of one dearly loved, for protection from some horrific experience, or for some other pressing need.

REMEMBER THE PRIORITY OF PRAYER

Prayer is to our spiritual lives what breathing is to our physical lives. Our breath draws something from outside us necessary for life. Breathing is an essential function. The unconscious rhythm of breathing provides life-sustaining oxygen. Its pace and intensity increase in times of special need. If you stop breathing, you will shrivel up and die.

Where spiritual life exists, prayer is a part of the rhythm of daily life. It draws sustaining power for our spirit. Moments of special need create a near sense of desperation—intensifying the pace and focus of prayer. Like physical breathing, if you stop praying, your spiritual life will experience a rapid decay.

Jesus was often in prayer. He departed from the crowds just to pray. He prayed at his most pressing moments. If the Son of God, who stopped the wind and waves, healed the blind and lame, and multiplied a few loaves to feed thousands, found it necessary to devote time to prayer, how much more so do we need to pray?

Jesus expected his followers to pray. He led them by example.

Jesus instructed his disciples how to pray (Matthew 6:5-15). He also specifically said we are to pray for the lost: "Pray earnestly to the Lord of the harvest to send out laborers into his harvest" (Matthew 9:38b).

In like manner, the apostles frequently prayed. They asked for prayer from those to whom they wrote. Scripture makes it plain prayer is an essential element of the Christian life. We are called to "pray without ceasing" (1 Thessalonians 5:17). Believers must recognize this and pray. It should be a part of the normal rhythm of our lives.

Like breathing, there are difficult moments when praying is hard. Several years ago, my life was placed in jeopardy by the mishap of a cardiologist during a heart procedure. Two days after discharge from the hospital, I developed difficulty breathing. An emergency trip to a local hospital revealed the sacs around my lungs were filling with fluid. Since I was on a blood thinner from my heart procedure, the medical team had to wait until its effects wore off before they could do two sequential procedures to drain the fluid from around my lungs. You can imagine that having to gasp for every breath for about eighteen hours while feeling I was suffocating produced a bit of anxiety. My wife sat beside my hospital bed, reminding me to breathe slowly and deeply, just as I had done for her during labor with the delivery of each of our children.

In like manner, times of deep despair can break the normal rhythm of prayer in our lives. At such times, we need reminders to slow down, breathe deeply, and pray. Sometimes we must push ourselves to do what we know we should, even if our heart seems unconvinced. It is a choice of the will to pray in the face of doubt. In such times, we should ask the Lord to dispel our unbelief (Mark 9:24).

This also points to one of the most helpful means by which we can minister to those in the grip of despair. People rarely know what to say at such times. Sometimes silence is best. Just be there. Your presence will help them feel anchored rather than that they are floating alone. Even better, hold their hand and lead them in prayer. In those moments of despair, put them on your shoulder and carry them with you to the throne of grace. Carry them as often as necessary, until they can once again make the journey themselves.

REMEMBER THE POWER OF PRAYER

The Bible declares one truth from beginning to end—prayer changes things. There is power in prayer!

> *The prayer of a righteous person has great power as it is working. Elijah was a man with a nature like ours, and he prayed fervently that it might not rain, and for three years and six months it did not rain on the earth. Then he prayed again, and heaven gave rain, and the earth bore its fruit.*
> **James 5:16b-18**

This is just one of many passages reminding us prayer makes a difference. We do not understand how the sovereignty of God and the appeals of men intertwine, but the Bible tells us God acts in response to the prayers of his people.

> *Therefore I tell you, whatever you ask in prayer, believe that you have received it, and it will be yours.*
> **Mark 11:24**

When one has not seen the answers that one hoped for, we need reminders that prayer does make a difference. Our experience in a particular need does not change the clear teaching of Scripture that the hand of God moves when we pray.

I have a close friend who has kept an in-depth prayer journal for many years. It has provided him with an evidence book that God answers prayer. Should doubt ever rise in his mind, he can review the many answers to prayer he has seen over the years. Perhaps you have no such written record, but in your times of doubt, you can surely recount many other prayers that God has answered, to remind yourself of prayer's power.

Remember the Call to be Persistent in Prayer

When one's prayer about a significant concern over a length of time meets with the silence of heaven, there is a temptation to throw in the towel and stop praying for the matter. Nevertheless, Jesus himself commended us to persist in our prayers:

> *And he told them a parable to the effect that they ought always to pray and not lose heart. He said, "In a certain city there was a judge who neither feared God nor respected man. And there was a widow in that city who kept coming to him and saying, 'Give me justice against my adversary.' For a while he refused, but afterward he said to himself, 'Though I neither fear God nor respect man, yet because this widow keeps bothering me, I will give her justice, so that she will not beat me down by her continual coming.' And the Lord said, "Hear what the unrighteous judge says. And will not God give justice to his elect, who cry to him day and night? Will he delay long over them? I tell you, he will give justice to them speedily. Nevertheless, when the Son of Man comes, will he find faith on earth?"*
> **Luke 18:1-8**

Jesus told this parable so his hearers might always pray and not lose heart. He understands our frustration when we appeal to heaven and hear no response. His instructions are rather simple—keep praying! Persist in prayer.

This is where the hard work of prayer meets its greatest demand. Continuing to ask when you see no answer is difficult. David experienced this challenge: "How long, O LORD? Will you forget me forever? How long will you hide your face from me?" (Psalm 13:1).

In this and other passages, the singer of Israel expressed his frustration at the failure of God to respond to his appeals. The pathos of his pain at the failure of God to move is clear. Perhaps we can find comfort in the reality that a man with a heart so tender toward God also experienced moments when he sensed the silence of heaven. More importantly, we can see the sovereign work of God through the span of David's life and know the Lord was at work—even when in the eyes of David, the Lord appeared unmoved. We can persist in prayer knowing that God is at work in our lives as well.

REMEMBER THE PROVIDENCE OF GOD IN PRAYER

We are to bring all our concerns to the Father. In the strong name of Jesus, we throw our petitions before the throne of the living God. Every burden on our heart is a legitimate petition to bring to our Father who is in heaven. It is good and right to persist in such petitions. However, we must also recognize the providence of God in this arena. Ask what you want, and do so with all earnestness. At the same time, we must remember God is sovereign concerning prayer. It is his rightful providence to determine how to answer and when.

God is all knowing and we are not. Do we really want God to answer our prayers in the way we feel is best, or in the way that our omniscient Father knows our prayers should be answered? Do we trust God enough to accept his will in answering our prayers?

The most earnest "unanswered" prayer ever raised to heaven flowed from the lips of our beloved Savior. His experience in the garden provides the greatest lesson for those struggling with the silence of heaven. In his experience, we can find the path to regain our confidence in prayer—even when our most important prayers meet with the silence of God.

> *And he withdrew from them about a stone's throw, and knelt down and prayed, saying, "Father, if you are willing, remove this cup from me. Nevertheless, not my will, but yours be done." And there appeared to him an angel from heaven, strengthening him. And being in agony he prayed more earnestly; and his sweat became like great drops of blood falling down to the ground.*
> **Luke 22:41-44**

I prayed fervently for my dear son's salvation. Despite this earnestness, even in my most intense moments of prayer, I never sweated great drops of blood. The force and agony of my prayer never reached this level. It did for Jesus. He pled with the Father to remove the cup he was about to drink. Yet the intensity and depth of his plea did not yield an escape from the awful cup of wrath he drank on our behalf. Are you grateful the Father did not grant the Son's plea in his moment of deep distress? If the Father had, there would be no hope for you and for me. Can we understand this? Can we grasp the wonderful truth that the Father's wisdom can be trusted in response to our prayers?

As Jesus hung on the cross, he faced the reality that his prayer requesting another path—avoiding the agony he now felt—was not granted. Still, in facing this realization amid his agony, what did he do? He once again prayed to the Father. He prayed that the Father not hold the soldiers' terrible deed against them (Luke 23:34). He then prayed commending his spirit into the Father's hands. The silence of heaven the night before did not restrain him from coming to the Father in prayer yet again. He did not do so with embittered resignation that the Father would have his way regardless of his prayers. No, he did so because he fully and unequivocally trusted the Father's choice. Indeed, he wanted the Father's will above his own. So must we.

Let us then with confidence draw near to the throne of
grace, that we may receive mercy and find grace to help
in time of need.
Hebrews 4:16

12

KEEPING YOUR HOPE IN HEAVEN

It was difficult to call our daughter and break the sad news. We waited until her husband came home, which would enable us to talk uninterrupted, and she could absorb the news without having to turn her attention immediately afterwards to her preschool children. What is the right way to tell your daughter that her brother, who was her closest playmate through their early years, was found dead from unknown causes by his landlord?

The response she and her husband gave made it clear they had prepared for this moment. Our son had escaped death numerous times over the years. Those who knew him best would not have been surprised to hear of his passing. Paramedics had resuscitated him yet again after an overdose just one month before his death. Our daughter and son-in-law had obviously considered in advance how they might give us hope when they received the phone call they felt was inevitable. When we spoke, they pointed us to heaven—the only place where we would find true hope and peace. Even more importantly, they pointed us to the God of heaven. They reminded us that when we cross the chasm of death and enter heaven ourselves, the glory of God will consume us—not the pain and questions about our son's life. All things arising in our hearts and minds right now will mean nothing when we stand in the presence of the glory of God.

Their words were what we needed to hear on that fateful day. We had spoken to many people after our son's death to inform them of the tragedy that had befallen our family. Some provided words of comfort, while others declared they did not know what to say. Many were more seasoned in their Christian walk, but none more spot-on in their words to us in that moment than our daughter.

Songwriter Andrew Peterson, in the perceptive words of his song entitled "Faith to be Strong" declares, "This life is not long, but it's hard."[23] We live in a fallen world. The beauty with which our Creator endowed his creation is marred—altered beyond measure. Nowhere is this more evident than in the pervasive sinful acts of man in our day. We live in a time when good is declared evil and evil called good. Yet we also see it in the physical hardship borne by many, the inexplicable natural disasters destroying indiscriminately, and the anguish of battling against our own flesh. In addition, the Christian life is a battle against foes more powerful than we can imagine (Ephesians 6:12). There is a reason Paul compares the Christian experience to that of a soldier or an athlete straining for a prize (Philippians 3:14). Yes, "This life is not long, but it's hard."

When the hardness of life seems so painfully present, we must take special care to keep our focus on the Father who gives us hope. We will not find hope in the creation that is so injured and marred by sin. We will not find it in people, experiences, or the natural world. Moreover, we will not find it in our children—no matter what path they choose. Nothing of this temporal realm will give us true hope. Yet we need hope to sustain us in the darkest moments of life.

While some mockingly speak of those who are so heavenly focused they are no earthly good, a true focus on heaven enables us to live this hard life in a manner wherein we can *be* of some earthly good. Most specifically, when our hope is in "our Father in heaven" (Matthew 6:9), how do we focus on our heavenly hope, even when we are jostled on the rocky road of life?

Focus Your Mind on Heaven

As in so many areas of the Christian life, right living requires right thinking. Being heavenly minded, having your hope in heaven, begins and is sustained by turning your mind to heaven. As the apostle Paul said, "Set your mind on things that are above,

---

23   Andrew Peterson, *After All These Years: A Collection,* © Centricity Music, 2014.

not on things that are on earth" (Colossians 3:2)

He is not suggesting you pay no attention to the road in front of you as you drive; he was a tentmaker and understood one needs to concentrate on the work at hand. Paul wasn't a pie-in-the-sky idealist. Yet think of all the things you focus your mind on throughout a normal day that have no bearing on the task before you. What topic (of no eternal value) do you find your mind wandering to throughout a normal day? Perhaps it is sports, food, or recreation. For just one day, try diverting your meditation to heaven when this fleeting topic comes to mind. I am confident you will be shocked by how much time you can devote to thinking about heaven.

Simply put, we *must* think about heaven. We need to make it a topic of our meditations. Begin by considering the picture of heaven that Scripture provides. The prophet Ezekiel, in the book bearing his name, and the apostle John in Revelation, provide us with the clearest glimpses of heaven. Many people, seeking fanciful interpretations, look for symbolism in the minutiae of the descriptions. It is helpful to remember that Ezekiel and John were seeking to describe things unseen on this earth. No words could describe the heavenly visions they beheld. Nothing in their experience could provide an accurate comparison. Nevertheless, the fundamental message of both writers is clear—they saw blazing glory almost painful to behold. Glorious. Glorious. Glorious. This is the portrait that was provided. Heaven is the place where the full glory of God radiates to unimaginable intensity. It *is* all about him! The marvelous truth is that all who place their faith in Jesus Christ will dwell there with him. This is our hope. Not our wish, but our confident assurance based upon the promises of our Savior himself. The portrait and the promise of heaven are topics on which we must set our minds.

Sadly, I am compelled to give a word of caution here. There are innumerable books written about heaven that are little more than fanciful musings and some are downright heretical. It boggles the mind to think of how many people create a picture of heaven based upon a so-called vision of a preschooler who claimed to have gone to heaven and returned. A fanciful notion of heaven will not create the hope that a confident assurance from the infallible Word of God provides. Discard the musings of those who seek to fill in the white spaces between the lines of Scripture. Keep your focus on what Scripture plainly tells us. There is plenty there to enrapture the hearts of true believers.

ALLOW HEAVEN TO CAPTURE YOUR HEART

You must give your heart over to a greater treasure than any earthly delight provides—even the delight of a human relationship. Mental anguish, sorrow, grief, remorse—all of these are expressions of our emotional selves. They can capture our hearts and draw us to dark places. In contrast, when the glory of heaven and the confident assurance of our citizenship there captivates us, it draws our heart out of those dark places and enables us to stand firm amid life's most painful moments. As one acquainted with both physical and emotional pain, the apostle Paul proclaimed,

> *So we do not lose heart. Though our outer nature is wasting away, our inner nature is being renewed day by day. For this slight momentary affliction is preparing for us an eternal weight of glory beyond all comparison, as we look not to the things that are seen but to the things that are unseen.*
> **2 Corinthians 4:16-18a**

Paul was not denying the hard realities of life. He was sensitive to the deep anguish people experience. This apostle knew suffering like few before or after him. He characterizes the affliction we experience as "light momentary affliction" because it is both momentary and light compared to the "eternal weight of glory" that will one day be ours. As we "weigh" the eternal glory we will experience, it places all suffering in this world into proper perspective. This hope of glory brings us comfort. Puritan pastor Richard Baxter declared, "Can a man be at a fire and not be warm; or in the sunshine and not have light? Can your heart be in heaven, and not have comfort?"[24]

---

24 Richard Baxter, William Orme. *The Practical Works of the Rev. Richard Baxter: With a Life of the Author, and a Critical Examination of His Writings. Volume 16,* (London: James Duncan, 1830), 225.

LET HEAVEN PERMEATE YOUR BEING

When our mind is set on heaven, when this hope captures our heart, we will be a people for whom the hope of heaven is the lens through which we filter all life experiences. Then we will truly see the world in which we live with an eternal perspective. When we have this perspective we will see the Father working, even in the most difficult moments of life.

Is all this simply a psychological trick to avoid pain by ignoring the hard realities of life? Is this just a mental escape technique? Is it perhaps, as Karl Marx said with derision, an opium to dull our senses? No, it is not. As John MacArthur in his book, *The Glory of Heaven*, put it, "We don't seek to escape this life by dreaming of heaven. But we do find we can endure this life because of the certainty of heaven." [25]

Life often overflows with hard things, including hard truths painful to bear. Loved ones of prodigals must cling to the portrait painted in the words of Scripture, assuring us that in heaven,

> *He will wipe away every tear from their eyes, and death*
> *shall be no more, neither shall there be mourning nor*
> *crying nor pain anymore, for the former things have*
> *passed away.*
> **Revelation 21:4**

How can this be true? How can the loss of my child and his absence from heaven not cause everlasting mourning in my heart? It brings me to tears now; why will it not do that for all eternity? Neither I nor anyone else on earth can answer those questions with certainty. Like most "how" questions, the answer resides in the mind of God alone. Nevertheless, we know it is true. Indeed, after making this declaration, the apostle John was told, "Write this down, for these words are trustworthy and true" (Revelation 21:5).

The one who is the Alpha and Omega has declared it so (v. 6). For this reason, you can rest in its certainty. Your only hope is in heaven. Set your mind there. Let heaven capture your heart,

---

25   John F. MacArthur. *The Glory of Heaven.* (Wheaton, Ill.: Crossway, 2013), 69.

until it permeates your being. It is then that you can face the hard things of life with true joy.

> *We always thank God, the Father of our Lord Jesus Christ ... because of the hope laid up for you in heaven.*
> **Colossians 1:3, 5**

13

LIVING WITH SADNESS

It was a surprisingly warm day in mid-March. The warmth compelled us to begin spring-cleaning early. Removal of the accumulated debris of fall and winter blown into the garage—as well as pitching a few items saved for too long—was the first order of business. As I hauled things outside to clear the floor and walls for sweeping, I bent over to pick up a football, then a street hockey puck, followed by a baseball mitt. Soon I was taking down the hockey sticks—all items I held with the thought that one day my son and I would again engage in these sporting activities together. No, it was more than a thought. It was a sincere wish that we would renew the years of enjoyment we shared in times past. We had spent so many hours together on roller blades in the street or with a ball in the yard. Now, it was certain this would never happen again.

As I placed these items among others to discard, the finality of my son's departure once again struck home. Soon, a profound sense of loss moved across my being. A sadness I could not shake engulfed me. As my wife returned from an errand and joined me in the task, she too experienced the grip of sadness. This had been our son's task for the preceding two years. A medical condition with my arms prohibited me from doing such chores. Our son accepted the offer to do the task with the agreement we would cover an expense of his in return. My wife had worked with him for the past two years and now, confronted with his absence, felt the permanency of his loss afresh. I asked, "Will the sadness ever go away?"

It is inevitable that those with a prodigal child who is estranged, or has departed this world, will experience periods of sadness. At times, the sadness will feel overwhelming. Sometimes it will be like a hidden weight you drag through the day—not enough to stop you in your tracks, but a burden weighing you down nonetheless. While not an experience unique to parents of prodigals, sadness is one of the more common and enduring realties such parents must face. Understanding and dealing with it is essential if one is to know peace.

WHY SADNESS COMES

Sadness is a visceral response to hard realities; it is the expression of a pained heart who has experienced a meaningful loss. Sometimes sadness is experienced over something you lost, while at other times it is something hoped for, yet never gained. For example, sadness is the experience of several women in Scripture who were barren (Genesis 18:12; 1 Samuel 1:5,10). Scripture also speaks of death as a loss causing sadness in need of comfort (Genesis 23:1-2, 24:67; Ruth 1:13; John 11:17-19).

Unlike depression, sadness is a normal and expected part of the cycle of life's experiences. It plays a productive role in helping us to remember what is important in life. Sadness can also point others to the reality of the moment. The Lord Jesus experienced sadness on numerous occasions. At the tomb of Lazarus (John 11:35, 38). At the failure of Jerusalem to come under his wing (Luke 13:34). At the wearying lack of faith in those with whom he ministered (Matthew 8:26). As he prepared to pray in the garden on the night of his betrayal, he declared, "My soul is very sorrowful, even to death" (Matthew 26:38). Such was the intensity of his sorrow! On each of these occasions his disciples perceived his sadness, which caused them to recognize the reality of the moment. After all, the prophet Isaiah portrays him as a man of sorrows (Isaiah 53).

Those with a prodigal should expect periods of sadness. Proverbs provides some frank assessments about the experiences of parents of a fool (which prodigals certainly exemplify):

> *A wise son makes a glad father, but a foolish son is a*
> *sorrow to his mother.*
> **Proverbs 10:1**

*A foolish son is a grief to his father and bitterness to her
who bore him.*
Proverbs 17:25

If you are the parent of a prodigal, you have experienced a loss, whether temporary or permanent. If your child has rejected the path you have taught him and embraced a ruinous lifestyle, you have experienced a meaningful loss. Something would be wrong if you did not have times of sadness.

It is unfortunate many have a poor reaction to a person who expresses sadness. We seem to get this intense need to deflect expressions of sadness and shake others out of this emotional response. "Cheer up," they say, "it's not so bad!" In reality, it is bad and you should be sad as well. After all, the Bible commends us to "weep with those who weep" (Romans 12:15).

Sadness will come upon you uninvited, prompted by things reminding you of your loss. Sadness will vary with intensity, both over time and with the things that provoke its presence. My mother died over twenty-five years ago, but I continue to feel a twinge of sadness every Mother's Day. In fact, the first twinge begins when I stand in the card aisle looking for a Mother's Day card for my wife. My wife has a winter coat that my mother wore (and yes, it looks great over twenty-five years later!). The first time I help her put the coat on each winter, I experience a sadness at the reminder of my mother's absence. It is less intense than during the early years, but it arises unexpectedly each year.

During our journey with our prodigal, it was not uncommon for memories or events to precipitate sadness over his broken condition. Sometimes it was a photo of a joyous family event from years past. Other times it was the memory of one of our son's humorous pithy sayings he spoke so frequently in his formative years. He could be downright hilarious and often left us in stitches. On other occasions, it was an event a "normal" family would have all their children attend. Some episodes of sadness surfaced in response to someone asking about our children, especially what each did for a living. Evading an awkward conversation (do you tell someone you just met that your son is in prison?) often left a backwash of sadness. Not too many weeks passed during our journey when something did not provoke at least momentary sadness.

After our son's death, I was surprised by how often visual cues provoked sadness. I cannot look at a bottle of ranch dressing without tears pooling in my eyes. Our son put ranch dressing on everything, except maybe ice cream. Just a glance at a bottle of this dressing sends my thoughts to him before I realize what is happening. My wife tears up each time she shops for groceries. Reminders of our son spring forth as she passes items on the shelves she used to purchase especially for him. Special places often provoke sadness—as they may be associated with a significant event you experienced with the loved one. A friend who lost two children is gripped with sadness at the sound of each of their favorite hymns, which he used to play for them on their piano. The provocation of sadness by such cues is a normal part of the pain of losing a loved one.

RESPONDING TO SADNESS

When a moment of unexpected sadness descends through a visual, auditory, or other reminder, those around us may struggle to understand our reaction. They may even worry something they said or did provoked the sadness. We can help them by letting them know we do not want to avoid such reminders, even when they bring a time of sadness. Whether sadness comes because of the prodigal's current plight or permanent loss, we do not want to forget them.

People sometimes confuse sadness and depression. While the differential diagnosis between normal sadness and depression remains a matter of debate among professionals, most health professionals and laymen alike recognize the two are not the same.[26] Sadness is a healthy response to a true loss. Being sad about everything and being unable to identify a precipitating factor is unhealthy, and most likely depression. Sadness focuses on a specific loss and is proportional to the loss. Depression dis-

26 Mario Maj. The continuum of depressive states in the population and the differential diagnosis between "normal" sadness and clinical depression. In: Jerome C. Wakefield, Steeves Demazeux (eds), *Sadness or Depression?: International Persepectives on the Depression Epidemic and Its Meaning,* (New York: Springer, 2016), 29-38.

torts the view we have of everything in life. While it is true a deep tragedy will cause a sadness that feels all consuming, and it may be for a short period, it is a transient response. Depression lingers for no obvious reason.[27]

Sadness, especially in response to death, becomes a problem when it is unremitting and impairs your ability to function. Most people are resilient and move beyond the immediate depth of grief. Some are held in its grip for an excessive period. Clinicians generally view grief that impairs normal functioning more than six months after the precipitating event, to require special intervention such as counseling.[28]

WHEN IN THE GRIP OF GRIEF

What do you do when you find yourself in a deep, dark valley and grief has overwhelmed you? How do you pull yourself up out of the abyss? You don't. Another must lift you out. This is why you must, as David expressed in Psalm 23, open your eyes and see the Lord in the midst of the shadows. You must speak scriptural truth to yourself, acknowledging that he has promised to be with you even in the darkest places. There's no place in which you are hidden from his sight. There's no crevice beyond his reach. As expressed so well by Bob Kauflin in his song "In the Valley," it is in this dark place where you can see him more clearly than ever:

> *When You lead me to the valley of vision*
> *I can see You in the heights*
> *And though my humbling wouldn't be my decision*
> *It's here Your glory shines so bright*
> *So let me learn that the cross precedes the crown*
> *To be low is to be high*
> *That the valley's where You make me more like Christ*
> *Let me find Your grace in the valley*

---

27 John Piper has provided one of the most helpful and concise treatments of this topic in his book, *When the Darkness Will Not Lift—Doing What We Can While We Wait for God—and Joy,* (Wheaton, Ill.: Crossway Books, 2006).

28 George A. Bonanno, *The Other Side of Sadness: What the New Science of Bereavement Tells Us About Life After Loss.* (New York: Basic Books, 2009), 110.

Let me find Your life in my death Let me find Your joy in my sor-
row Your wealth in my need
That You're near with every breath In the valley

In the daytime there are stars in the heavens
But they only shine at night
And the deeper that I go into darkness
The more I see their radiant light
So let me learn that my losses are my gain
To be broken is to heal
That the valley's where Your power is revealed
Let me find Your grace in the valley
Let me find Your life in my death
Let me find Your joy in my sorrow
Your wealth in my need
That You're near with every breath
In the valley.[29]

The words of this song, and Psalm 23, have been a solace to my soul in the darkest moments of grief. No person could shake me out of grief. The Lord had to open my eyes, so I could see him in the midst of the darkness. I also needed to know my experience was not interminable. Psalm 40 expresses the experience of David in the midst of darkness:

> *I waited patiently for the LORD; he inclined and heard my cry. He drew me up from the pit of destruction, out of the miry bog, and set my feet upon a rock, making my steps secure. He put a new song in my mouth, a song of praise to our God. Many will see and fear, and put their trust in the LORD.*
> **Psalm 40:1-3**

We do not know how long David wallowed in the miry bog. But we do know he did not remain there. God does not leave his children destitute of his comfort. He will come. So, we wait

---

29   Music and words by Bob Kauflin. Based on *The Valley of Vision* prayer "The Valley of Vision" by Arthur Bennett © 2006 Sovereign Grace Praise (BMI). Sovereign Grace Music, a division of Sovereign Grace Churches. All rights reserved.

patiently for his delivering arms to reach down and draw us out.

This also guides us on how we can minister to another who is in the strong grip of grief. You cannot shake them out of it. But you can intercede on their behalf and plead like Elijah, "O LORD, please open his eyes that he may see" (2 Kings 6:17). Like Job's three companions who began mourning with their friend, just be there with them. But be careful when you open your mouth—lest you repeat the folly of Job's friends. Speak biblical truth to nourish their soul. But do so with great gentleness and love.

What do we do while the grip of grief still holds us as we wait for the Lord? First, we must nourish our soul. The primary source of nourishment should be the Scriptures. The Psalms overflow with soul-bearing experiences that can bring hope in times of turmoil. They remind us of the Good Shepherd's care for his sheep in their times of need. Music can also be a healing balm. Listen to hymns and songs proclaiming Scriptural truth. Let the melodies draw your heart upward.

Second, we need the fellowship of other believers. Sometimes trauma knocks us off our feet. Our son's running away from home as a teenager, his first arrest, his imprisonment, our decision not to take him in when he was homeless, and especially his death; each sent shock waves into our world. Part of us wanted to hibernate in our home to avoid the inevitable questions and awkward words of others. Adding embarrassment to our sadness didn't seem helpful.

But we needed others to help us regain our footing. It was hard to sing praises to God in such moments. Yet the joyous voices of the congregation of God's people carried us to the throne through their songs. And the preaching of the Word drew us to where our hearts needed to be.

Third, we must do what needs to be done. Early on, we may find ourselves like Job—fully consumed by grief. During the initial days of grief, other activities may need to be set aside until your feet are once again on steady ground. But then, we must move forward and do what needs to be done while we wait for the Lord. In one of the Songs of Ascent, the psalmist declares,

> *Those who sow in tears shall reap shouts of joy!*
> *He who goes out weeping, bearing the seed for sowing,*
> *shall come home with shouts of joy,*
> *bringing his sheaves with him.*
> **Psalm 126:5-6**

This psalm is a promise for restoration. There is a window of time in which seed must be sown. Sowing cannot wait for the farmer to feel up to doing it. The need cannot be set aside because of other things, even painful losses. The farmer must go forth and sow even when weighed down by sadness to the point of tears. But the promise is that days of joy are ahead. Even in grief, we must do what must be done. We pick ourselves up and fulfill our duties as spouses, parents, employees, and laborers in the Lord's fields.

For my wife, returning to her role of leading our church's ministry to the homeless presented an incredible challenge. Every day on her drive to and from the shelter for the homeless, she passed by the house in which our son died and also the funeral home which we used. She would enter a room highly populated with clients like our son—people who had given themselves to reckless living. Many had a mother somewhere who prayed for them through their tears. The initial weeks of returning to this work were distressing to her soul. Yet she went forward and did what needed to be done. On occasion, she had to pull over to let the tears flow before resuming her drive home.

Deep sadness does not bring life to a screeching halt. It may slow things down for a moment. But there comes a time to press on despite the continued pain. We do so knowing that grief is for a season. As the psalmist declares elsewhere, "Weeping may tarry for the night, but joy comes with the morning" (Psalm 30:5).

I don't believe the psalmist was putting a twelve-hour limit on our time of weeping. He used poetic language to remind us that grief does not last for an interminable period. It is for a season. Though the season of this experience may vary in length, the sorrow will end one day.

Words of Caution

A word of caution is needed for those who find themselves in the strong grip of grief, as well as those who counsel or otherwise minister to them. Believers must be careful about judging the spiritual maturity or vibrancy of their own or another's faith during experiences of despair. Would God characterize you or me in the exemplary manner in which he regarded Job? Yet the emotional and physical battering Job experienced left him in a state of despair. Would any of us be bold enough to equate our walk with the Lord with David's walk (whom God declared to be a man after his own heart)? Nevertheless, the Psalms provide many examples of despondency in David's life. None of us have experienced the power of the Spirit working miraculously through us in the manner of Elijah, yet this prophet of God gave way to despair.

The enemy of our soul, combined with the weakness of our corruptible flesh, can grab hold of even giants of the faith. If a man like Charles Haddon Spurgeon, often called the Prince of Preachers, could be plagued with repeated periods of the deep darkness of despondency, should we be surprised when we are gripped in like manner?[30] Do not question the faith of someone simply because an unshakable darkness has descended upon them.

You should be concerned if sustained sadness arises from continual brooding over your loss. Some cling to possessions and try to ignore that life has changed through their loss. For example, some parents refuse to alter a departed child's room—leaving it exactly as it was. Responses of this nature are unhealthy and set one on the dangerous road of turning the memories of the departed into a shrine.

Husbands need to take special care. Mothers tend to be more sensitive to sentimental reminders. Who would honestly deny that carrying a child for nine months, and subsequent months of

---

30 I would commend to the reader *Steal Away Home* by Matt Carter and Aaron Ivey (Nashville, Tenn. B&H Publishing, 2017). The authors masterfully weave the account of the lives of C.H. Spurgeon and Thomas Johnson—a wise former American slave who the Lord used over the years to deliver Spurgeon from the darkness that repeatedly descended upon his life. There is much counselors can learn from this account.

nursing, creates a deeper bond than any father experiences? Your wife may experience more episodes of sadness than you do, and with greater intensity. Give her space to have emotional responses differing from yours. She needs your understanding and support during these times. Just hold her in your arms and weep with her.

The sadness of the passing of a prodigal presents special challenges because it is inextricably linked to their eternal loss. There is nothing more painful for a parent. I am convinced this pain will never fully pass until we enter eternity. How could it? It would be unthinkable that this reality would not provoke sadness. As quoted earlier, Proverbs 17:25 tells us that "a foolish son is a grief to his father and bitterness to her who bore him." While true in life, it is even more so in death. In the early days after our son's death, facing this reality was tortuous. And at times, it remains so. I have found only one remedy for the deep distress such moments produce. Specifically, to remember the Lord is who one grieves most. He has experienced myriads rejecting the saving offer of his Son. He gave the ultimate price, but most who tread this earth reject his gracious offer. Innumerable people through the ages have chosen perdition, rather than his gracious offer. Every year, every decade, every century, every millennium since God placed man on this earth, most have chosen to turn from him (Matthew 7:13). What could be more painful? His pain is truly greater than mine.

Sadness is expected when we experience loss. Reminders of the loss will understandably bring new periods of sadness. What is unhealthy is ruminating on the loss, becoming obsessed, and allowing it to be the focal point of our lives. John Piper said it well: "Occasionally weep deeply over the life you hoped would be. Grieve the losses. Then wash your face. Trust God. And embrace the life you have."[31]

> Why am I discouraged? Why is my heart so sad? I will
> put my hope in God! I will praise him again – my Savior
> and my God!
> **Psalm 42:11 NLT**

---

31   John Piper, *Embrace the Life God Has Given You.* Desiring God Ministries, www.desiring-god.org, video posted March 10, 2017.

14

TESTING THE SUFFICIENCY OF HIS GRACE

I had to sit down. Overwhelmed with a sense of impending doom, my legs almost gave way. An approaching tsunami was racing towards me, about to destroy everything I held dear. I could only wait for it to crash ashore and wreak its havoc on my life. Nothing would prevent its arrival. Its presence was imminent. Only dread filled the time before it overtook me.

Moments earlier, I received a call on my cell phone. "Is this the father of Eric Svensson?" the caller asked. After affirming I was, he said he was calling from the county coroner's office and asked if we could meet somewhere. I asked, "What is this about, what has happened?" "Well," he said, "I don't like to do this by phone, but we have found a body and think it may be your son. I'd like to bring you some pictures to look at. Where could we meet?" How does one answer such a question? I gave him directions to my office at the university and awaited his arrival.

Words cannot express the wave of emotion that swept over me as I waited for this unknown gentleman from the coroner's office. Our son's reckless behavior brought repeated brushes with death. My wife and I had often felt the day would come when we would bury our son. Despite years of this anticipation, when the fateful event unfolded in real time, the weight of gloom that overtook me became almost unbearable. If I had been standing on the edge of a precipice, I may well have jumped in a foolish attempt to escape the inevitable. The fifteen minutes he took to arrive at my office were the most anxious minutes of my life. I probably aged years in those moments.

This book began with the moment when I learned that the body they found was indeed our son. From there, I rushed home to the most difficult task I have ever had to fulfill in my life— telling my wife our precious son was gone. Only divine protection explains how I drove home through torrential tears and desperate agony of soul without causing an accident. I felt as though all the air had escaped my lungs as I told my wife of our son's death. Then came the fullness of the horror, as we were seized with the anguish that our son, by all indications, perished without Christ. The next twenty-four hours were an absolute torture to our souls. Speaking the words of his death repeatedly, as we called family and friends for hours on end, heaped pain upon pain. It all seemed so overwhelming, more than we could possibly bear. But it wasn't.

Over time, we learned the same thing we had experienced in other trials—God's grace is sufficient. We embraced this biblical truth long ago, but now learned it again through tragedy. Learned is perhaps a poor choice of words. We tested the truth of Scripture and found it to be true. He does provide "grace to help in time of need" (Hebrews 4:16b). Grace sufficient for our need.

An Exhibit of the Sufficiency of Grace

None declared so plainly, nor showed with such power, the sufficiency of God's grace in times of need than the apostle Paul. After reminding the Roman believers "that for those who love God all things work together for good, for those who are called according to his purpose" (Romans 8:28), he went on to say,

> *Who shall separate us from the love of Christ? Shall tribulation, or distress, or persecution, or famine, or nakedness, or danger, or sword? As it is written, "For your sake we are being killed all the day long; we are regarded as sheep to be slaughtered." No, in all these things we are more than conquerors through him who loved us.*
> **Romans 8:35-37**

Not victims, but conquerors. No distress will defeat those in

Christ. No depth of anguish will cause our souls to perish. A man who knew the depths of suffering penned these words. Consider the catalogue of his experience:

> ... more imprisonments, with countless beatings, and often near death. Five times I received at the hands of the Jews the forty lashes less one. Three times I was beaten with rods. Once I was stoned. Three times I was shipwrecked; a night and a day I was adrift at sea; on frequent journeys, in danger from rivers, danger from robbers, danger from my own people, danger from Gentiles, danger in the city, danger in the wilderness, danger at sea, danger from false brothers; in toil and hardship, through many a sleepless night, in hunger and thirst, often without food, in cold and exposure.
> **2 Corinthians 11:23-27**

All that Paul endured is unfathomable to us. We have not been pressed so far, nor experienced such extremes. But if we had, we could bear it just as he did. For it was not Paul's personal strength that enabled him to endure, but the sufficiency of God's grace—a grace available to all who are a part of God's forever family. Paul goes on in this letter to the saints at Corinth to say,

> a thorn was given to me in the flesh, a messenger of Satan to harass me, to keep me from being conceited. Three times I pleaded with the Lord about this, that it should leave me. But he said to me, "My grace is sufficient for you, for my power is made perfect in weakness."
> **2 Corinthians 12:7-9**

Paul felt impaled by this messenger of Satan (the word refers to a wooden stake, not the thorn of a bush). The acuity and depth of his suffering is unmistakable. Nevertheless, Paul knew that times of weakness in the face of distress were an opportunity for God's grace to be on special display. Knowing this, Paul declared,

> *Therefore I will boast all the more gladly of my weaknesses, so that the power of Christ may rest upon me. For the sake of Christ, then, I am content with weaknesses, insults, hardships, persecutions, and calamities. For when I am weak, then I am strong.*
> **2 Corinthians 12:9b-10**

For those who feel the fate of your prodigal is more than you can possibly bear, I tell you it is not. Yes, it is deeply painful. Tortuous at times. You may think that the burden will crush you. But it will not. We have seen and experienced the sufficiency of the grace of which the apostle Paul testified. We have watched it lived out in the lives of other parents of prodigals. You can rest upon this sure promise.

Grace Sufficient for Our Trials

Sixteen months before our son's death, I entered the hospital for a cardiac procedure to treat a persistent arrhythmia to which I alluded in chapter eleven. Toward the end of the six-hour procedure, the cardiologist inadvertently and unknowingly poked a hole in the upper chamber of my heart. This resulted in blood filling the sac around my heart, which required a life-saving emergency procedure hours later, as I descended into cardiogenic shock. A tube was placed allowing this sac to drain excess blood and assure that none accumulated internally. About one hour after its removal the following day, I experienced crushing chest pain. I have experienced intense pain at other times in my life, but none like this. It was as though an eighteen-wheel tractor-trailer had parked on my chest—its weight pressing deeper and deeper into my thoracic cavity. I erroneously surmised it was a heart attack, one likely to end my earthly journey. I did not expect to survive a massive heart attack so few hours after being rescued from cardiogenic shock. The intensity of pain was so great I did not believe I could bear it another minute. I was about to pray, asking the Lord to just take me home. Looking over at the face of my anxious wife, I realized answering my request would cause her deep and abiding sadness. Instead, I prayed for the strength to bear this unbelievable pain that seemed to be draining my life away. My prayer was granted. I endured more pain than I believed possible.

Weeks into my recuperation from the cardiac ordeal, a young pastor asked what I learned during my trial. Among other things, I told him I discovered that I could endure more acute physical pain than I ever thought possible. I would not have known this apart from a journey to the edge of my pain tolerance.

For readers whose children have come to tragic ends, I know you think the burden you now face is even greater than the one you bore during their earthly existence. It seems to you that it is a burden too great to bear. This is because you have never been there before. You did not need such an abounding measure of grace. Now you do. God promises to supply all your needs. His grace truly is sufficient for the moment in which you dwell.

By God's design, in the weeks leading up to our son's death, our daughter worked on writing a new arrangement of the classic hymn "His Grace Is Enough for Me." She recorded it and sent it to us soon after his death. In the days that followed, despite the agony and depth of pain through which we walked, we found that its message rang true:

> *When I am disheartened,*
> *With cares oppressed,*
> *When my way is darkest,*
> *When I am distressed—*
> *My Savior is near me,*
> *He knows my every care;*
> *Jesus will not leave me,*
> *He helps my burdens bear.*
>
> *His grace is enough for me,*
> *His grace is enough for me;*
> *Through sorrow and pain,*
> *Through loss or gain,*
> *His grace is enough for me.*

When my hopes are vanished,
When my friends forsake,
Just when the fight is thickest,
With fear I shake—
There's a still small whisper:
"Fear not, My child, I'm near."
Jesus brings me comfort,
I love His voice to hear
His grace is enough for me,
His grace is enough for me;
Through sorrow and pain,
Through loss or gain,
His grace is enough for me.

When my tears are flowing,
Just when with anguish bent,
When my temptation's hardest,
With sadness rent—
There's a thought of comfort:
"I know my Father knows."
His grace is sufficient
To conquer all my foes.
His grace is enough for me,
His grace is enough for me;
Through sorrow and pain,
Through loss or gain,
His grace is enough for me.[32]

It is true. His grace is enough for you. My wife and I have experienced it in our lives. To be honest, early on we did not know how we could bear life having had a son who perished without evidence of repentance. The torture in our souls was more excruciating than any physical or emotional pain we had ever known. Nevertheless, we have found God's grace is enough. We have watched others journey on unbelievably painful paths. Each time when tested, his grace has proved to be enough. You need

---

32 Original by J. Bruce Evans, 1906; Arrangement by Kate Craig ©2017.

not fear that you will be the first in human history to find his grace insufficient for your need.

> *My grace is sufficient for you, for my power is made*
> *perfect in weakness.*
> **2 Corinthians 12:9**

The Painful Path of a Prodigal

15

A FINAL WORD

The official notice came late on a Thursday afternoon. Four weeks had passed since we learned of our son's death. My plan was to travel to Boston the next day to receive an honored recognition. I arrived home with my mind focused on what I needed to pack for my trip. Walking into our kitchen, I found my precious wife seated at our breakfast nook in tears, with a torn envelope on the counter and an official form on top. I wrapped her in my arms and, after a time of comforting, looked down at the form. It was our son's death certificate that had just arrived in the mail. In the coldest fashion, we learned the coroner's assessment of our son's death. My eyes raced through the form looking for the determined cause of death. There were no specific clues at the scene when his body was found. Finding the dreadful words, my heart sank. Sepsis and gastrointestinal bleeding. My clinical experience told me his last hours, and probably days, must have been ones of misery. Within me there arose the painful question: Why? Why did he not seek help? Why did he not seek medical attention? He never hesitated to do so in the past. In recent years, he was a frequent user of our local EMT service. So, why did he not do so when there was a rapid and serious decline in his health?

My mind raced back to a conversation one month before his death. He lay in the back seat of my SUV as I drove him ninety minutes south of our town to a medical appointment. It was with a surgeon who had done multiple reconstructive surgeries on his knee following an accident—one resulting from his reckless behavior. He had long resisted any spiritual conversation, and on this occasion it was no different. But this did not prevent our persistent efforts to focus him on his true need in life. Gently and lovingly, we sought always to point him to the only path of true healing. I don't recall our exact words to one another, but I will never forget the overall assessment he gave of himself—"Perhaps, I am beyond hope." I assured him that as long as he had breath there was, from a human perspective, still hope. Then he fell silent—the conversation stopped.

Had he failed to seek help because he had given up all hope? Had he lost the will to live because he saw no escape from his self-inflicted misery? We will never know the answer to this and other related questions, but they have continued to arise whenever I think about our fifteen-year journey with our prodigal. Those heart-rending questions also serve as a compelling motivation for this final word. If I could leave you with one word of advice on dealing with your prodigal, it would be this: Continually hold hope before him. Let him know there is a path to escape the destructive road he is on. Yes, the journey will be hard for him. Nevertheless, in Christ, it can be done and you will be at his side for the journey.

Despair, whatever its cause, can be life-draining. In our work with the homeless over the years, my wife and I have often seen the look of despair on the faces of clients. Unless one has seen it and personally experienced it, the depth of the destructive impact of giving one's life over to a path of sin is hard to comprehend. Lives are quickly messed up, and setting things on the right path may seem like trying to unscramble an egg.

By definition, a prodigal is one who has seen what the path of righteousness looks like when lived out on this earth. He was in a family who experienced the blessing of walking with the Lord and the attendant joy accompanying the path of righteousness. He has seen up close what it means to be planted by a stream of living water. Despite this experience, he has chosen to depart from this path and walk in the way of the ungodly. He has chosen to sit in the seat of scoffers. As such, he sees the contrast that those who are not prodigals will never see. In addition, if he truly sees, he will recognize the depths of darkness into which he has fallen. In a sense, he has had a taste of what he is missing by his evil choices. Without seeing a visible path of escape, he will fall into the depths of despair unmatched by those who have never seen the righteous path.

History is replete with stories of men and women who have triumphed in the midst of the most trying of circumstances. The common thread in their lives is hope. Whether something better was near or far away, hope enabled them to keep pressing on in the midst of their trials.

We serve a God who delights in redeeming broken lives. He is so passionate about doing so that he sent his son to pay the unthinkable price for sinners, in order to bring them into his forever family. The offer of this redemption is to be shared with all people. The experience of redemption does not mean one's problems will all disappear and the temporal consequences of years of evil choices will be wiped away. But it does mean that one can be set on a new path, a path whose route and end will differ greatly from the one on which the prodigal is currently travelling. We must do whatever it takes to hold this hope before them. We must remind them repeatedly that the offer is theirs for the taking.

Come to me, all who labor and are heavy laden, and I will give you rest.
Matthew 11:28

ACKNOWLEDGMENTS

Writing may be a solitary endeavor, but producing a book is a collective activity. No one deserves greater thanks in making this book than my beloved wife, Sue. No man has ever had a better life partner. We journeyed together on the hard road described in this book. The process of writing and revising added tears and anguish of soul for us both. I am immeasurably grateful for her willingness to bear this added burden because of the deep desire to help others. I will never understand why I am the object of her unwavering love, but I gladly give her mine.

Our daughter Kate bore the burden of a prodigal sibling, as well as the anguish of watching her parents try to figure out how to help him. Her young life was harder than we would have hoped by both his and our struggles on this undesirable road. We are grateful that Christ captured her heart at a young age. Highlights of joy in her life often helped us bear the most difficult valleys. I am grateful for her willingness that I include her in parts of this story, in addition to reproducing her arrangement of "His Grace is Enough for Me."

A number of individuals were generous with their time— reading and commenting on various drafts. Brent Aucoin was especially gracious in providing several critical reads. Among other help, his feedback prompted the application section in chapter 2. Bob Kellemen kindly gave his experience and time to advise this novice author. Other helpful reviewers include Jocelyn Wallace, Pam Gannon, Sandy Fink, and Charles Hodges. They have made this a better book. The remaining deficiencies most likely arise from my failure to heed their advice.

I am also indebted to authors who have written about various types of suffering. In particular, C. S. Lewis, Joni Eareckson Tada, and Timothy Keller. They have helped me to think biblically about the agony of soul often arising with suffering, and the sovereignty of God in the midst of agony. Many other authors, preachers, and teachers have been used by God in my personal growth. Their ideas and phrases have surely found a lodging place in my mind, though the origins of such words are now lost to my memory. Those that have appeared in this book without acknowledgment do so without any intent for my part to take credit for the ideas of others. Like many, I have probably never had an original thought and merely stand on the shoulders of others.

Thanks is due to the shepherds who pastored us well during the years of our difficult journey—Tim Waldron, Steve Viars, and Brent Aucoin. May the Chief Shepherd bless them for their kindness. The congregation of Evangel Community Church was a special blessing during my three years as their interim preacher, as they upheld us in the early years of our painful journey.

I am immensely grateful for the fine folks at Shepherd Press for believing in this project. Jim Holmes was of much encouragement as he guided the process of turning the manuscript into a book. Rick and Bonnie Irvin went above and beyond their editorial duties, providing compassionate understanding as we engaged in the process of refining the text and typesetting it and then selecting a cover image. Andy Heckathorne provided a thoughtful cover design for a difficult topic.

Our love for our dear son endured through very difficult years. Although I have shared openly painful episodes of his life in this book, readers would be mistaken if they doubt our love for him. A part of us would like to hide the dark side of his life. But I have shared these episodes in the earnest hope that the Lord might in some way use our candor to help others—for our Lord specializes in exchanging "beauty for ashes." Our memory of Eric will be richer if recounting parts of our shared journey is of help to others.

ABOUT THE AUTHOR

Craig K. Svensson, PharmD, PhD, is Dean Emeritus of Pharmacy and Professor of Medicinal Chemistry & Molecular Pharmacology at Purdue University, as well as Adjunct Professor of Pharmacology & Toxicology at the Indiana University School of Medicine. He has served as a Bible Teacher, interim preacher, a seminary board chair, a mission agency board chair, small group leader, and as visiting lecturer at the Bryansk Bible Institute and Seminary in Bryansk, Russia. He and his wife of thirty-five years live in West Lafayette, IN, where they serve with Faith Church. He is the author of *When There Is No Cure: How to Thrive While Living with the Pain and Suffering of Chronic Illness.*

Visit CraigSvensson.com

BIBLIOGRAPHY

Bailey, Kenneth E. *The Cross & the Prodigal: Luke 15 Through the Eyes of Middle Eastern Peasants*. 2nd Edition, IVP Books, 2005.

Baxter, Richard and Orme, William. *The Practical Works of the Rev. Richard Baxter: With a Life of the Author, and a Critical Examination of His Writings*. Volume 23. James Duncan, 1830.

Bonanno, George A. *The Other Side of Sadness: What the New Science of Bereavement Tells Us About Life After Loss*. Basic Books, 2009.

Coleman, Bill. *Parents with Broken Hearts: Helping Parents of Prodigals to Cope*. Revised Edition, BMH Books, 2007.

Fee, Gordon D. and Stuart, Douglas. *How to Read the Bible for All Its Worth*. Zondervan, 1981.

Graham, Ruth Bell. *Prodigals and Those Who Love Them*. Baker Book House, 1999.

Harvey, Dave, Gilbert, Paul. *Letting Go: Rugged Love for Wayward Souls*. Zondervan, 2016.

Keller, Timothy J. *Walking with God through Pain and Suffering*. Penguin Books, 2013.

Lewis, Margie M. with Lewis, Gregg. *The Hurting Parent: Help and Hope for Parents of Prodigals*. Revised and Expanded, Zondervan, 2000.

Lloyd-Jones, Martyn. *Joy Unspeakable: Power & Revival in the Holy Spirit*, Harold Shaw Publishers, 1984.

MacArthur, John F. *The MacArthur New Testament Commen-*

tary: Matthew 1-7. Moody Press, 1985.

MacArthur, John F. *The MacArthur New Testament Commentary: 1 Peter*. Moody Publishers, 2004.

MacArthur, John F. *The Gospel According to Jesus: What Is Authentic Faith? Revised and Expanded Anniversary Edition*, Zondervan, 2008.

MacArthur, John F. *The Glory of Heaven: The Truth About Heaven, Angels, and Eternal Life. 2nd Edition*, Crossway, 2013.

MacArthur, John F. *Parables: The Mysteries of God's Kingdom Revealed Through the Stories Jesus Told*. Thomas Nelson, 2015.

MacDonald, James. *Come Home: A Call Back to Faith*. Moody Publishers, 2013.

Maj, Mario. The continuum of depressive states in the population and the differential diagnosis between "normal" sadness and clinical depression. In: Jerome C. Wakefield, Steeves Demazeux (eds), *Sadness or Depression*, Springer, pp. 29-38, 2016.

Packer, J.I. *Evangelism & the Sovereignty of God*. IVP, 1961.

Packer, J.I. *Knowing God*. IVP, 1973.

Packer, J.I. *A Quest for Godliness: The Puritan Vision of the Christian Life*. Crossway, 1990.

Parsons, Greg W. *Guidelines for understanding and proclaiming the book of Proverbs*. Bibliotheca Sacra 150:151-170, 1993.

Putman, Jim with Putman, Bill. *Hope for the Prodigal: Bringing the Lost, Wandering, and Rebellious Home*. Baker Books, 2017.

Sproul, R.C. *Chosen By God: Know God's Perfect Plan for His Glory and His Children*. Tyndale House Publishers, 1986.

Spurgeon, Charles H. *Early Religious Impressions*, https://www.spurgeon.org/resource-library/books/ix-early-religious-impressions#flipbook/3

Tozer, A.W. *I Call It Heresy!* Christian Publications, 1991.

Wright, H. Norman. *Loving Your Rebellious Child: A Survival Guide for Parents of Prodigals*. Authentic Publishers, 2013.

Resources

Suggested reading:

Emlet, Michael R. *Descriptions and Prescriptions: A Biblical Perspective on Psychiatric Diagnosis & Medications*. Prodigals who encounter the medico-legal system will inevitably be labeled with some form of mental health diagnosis. This helpful primer by physician and biblical counselor Michael Emlet can help parents think about these complex issues from a biblical framework.

Harvey, Dave and Gilbert, Paul. *Letting Go: Rugged Love for Wayward Souls*. Zondervan, 2016. Harvey and Gilbert provide one of the most helpful books on dealing with the hard choices faced by those with prodigals.

Jones, Robert D. *Prodigal Children: Hope and Help for Parents*. P&R Publishing, 2018. In this booklet, Robert Jones provides a brief and compassionate guide for parents dealing with the pain of a prodigal child. Biblical counselors would do well to have this available as a first read for counselees with prodigals.

Kellemen, Robert W. *God's Healing for Life's Losses: How to Find Hope When You're Hurting*. BMH Books, 2010. With honesty and compassionate understanding, Kellemen can help those impacted by a prodigal, or other trauma, move from "hurt to hope in Christ."

Piper, John. *When the Darkness Will Not Lift: Doing What We*

Can While We Wait for God–and Joy, Crossway Books, 2006. With his usual insightful and pastoral compassion, John Piper helps those gripped by darkness (such as may come on parents of prodigals), as well as those who would seek to minister to them.

Viars, Stephen. *Putting Your Past In Its Place: Moving Forward in Freedom and Forgiveness*. Harvest House Publishers, 2011. Dealing with past hurts can be one of the most important issues that family members of prodigals (and prodigals themselves) must face. I know of no better resource to guide one to a Christlike response to the pain of the past than Steve Viars' helpful book.

DEVOTIONALS AND PRAYER GUIDES FOR PARENTS OF PRODIGALS:

Graham, Ruth Bell. *Prodigals and Those Who Love Them*. Baker Book House, 1999.

Guthrie, Nancy (Ed). *Be Still My Soul: Embracing God's Purpose & Provision in Suffering*. Crossway, 2010.

Idleman, Kyle. *Praying for Your Prodigal*. David C. Cook, 2014.

Morgan, Robert J. *Prayers and Promises for Worried Parents*. Howard Books, 2003.

ORGANIZATIONS PROVIDING HELPFUL RESOURCES:

Biblical Counseling Coalition. https://biblicalcounselingcoalition.org/

Parents of Prodigals. http://www.parentsofprodigals.com/

Prodigal Child Ministries. http://www.prodigalchildministries.org/